Dedication

To Neil Barsky, Jim Fishel, David Jones, Bill Josephson, and Lee Kravitz—five men who have generously supported Youth Communication's work to train, inform, and educate teens.

Acknowledgments

The *Real Men* project was made possible by the generous support of the Pinkerton Foundation, the Charles Hayden Foundation, and the Campaign for Black Male Achievement at the Open Society Institute.

In addition, more than 30 other foundations and hundreds of individuals supported the workshops in which the stories in *Real Men* were written.

Thanks to Sean Chambers, Vinny Daverso, Kenneth Douglas, Rodney Fuller, Monte Givhan, Pauline Gordon, Sheridan Honore, and Ferentz Lafargue for providing early feedback on organization and content.

Finally, thank you to the 26 young men who courageously told the stories that appear in this book. Special thanks to Troy Shawn Welcome and Antwaun Garcia for their extraordinary contributions.

The Authors

Joseph
Alvarez

Derrick B.

Norman B.

Sharif
Berkeley

Robin Chan

Macario
DeLaCruz

Antwaun
Garcia

Eric Green

Jamal Green

Otis Hampton

Curtis Holmes

Ashunte Hunt

Gamal Jones

Ferentz
LaFargue

Juelz Long

Edgar Lopez

Michael Orr

Xavier Reyes

Manny S.

Stephen
Simpson

Jeremiyah
Spears

Jordan
Temple

Fred
Wagenhauser

Troy Shawn
Welcome

Jordan Yue

Real Men
Real Stories

Urban Teens Write
About How to Be a Man

By Youth Communication

Edited by Laura Longhine

Read. Write. Succeed.

Real Men Real Stories

Executive Editors
Keith Hefner and Laura Longhine

Contributing Editors
Nora McCarthy, Phil Kay, Rachel Blustain, Andrea Estepa, Kendra Hurley, Hope Vanderberg, Sheila Feeney, Tamar Rothenberg, Al Desetta, Sasha Chavkin, Virginia Vitzthum

Layout & Design
Efrain Reyes and Jeff Faerber

Cover Art
YC Art Dept.
Thanks to cover model James "Jamel" Bodrick

For reprint information, please contact Youth Communication.

ISBN 978-1-935552-43-7

First Edition
Printed in the United States of America

Youth Communication ®
New York, New York
212-279-0708
www.youthcomm.org

Catalog Item #YD-RM

"When we're young, it sometimes seems like the world doesn't exist outside our city, our block, our house, our room. We make decisions based on what we see in that limited world and follow the only models available. The most important thing that happened to me...was that I found myself surrounded by people...who kept pushing me to see more than what was directly in front of me, to see the boundless possibilities of the wider world and the unexplored possibilities within myself. People who taught me that no accident of birth—not being black or relatively poor, being from Baltimore or the Bronx or fatherless—would ever define or limit me. In other words, they helped me to discover what it means to be free."

—Wes Moore
Rhodes Scholar, combat veteran,
and author of *The Other Wes Moore*

Foreword

by Geoffrey Canada

Who are the boys in this book? Young men of color, presented in a clear-eyed way that is rare to find these days. Young men of color are a presence in the media and public consciousness as never before—but, unfortunately, they are usually not shown in a positive light. Gangster rappers and trash-talking athletes are often the spokesmen and role models for this generation of young men, reinforcing the fearful stereotypes of the larger society—and the low expectations the young men have for themselves.

The fact that hundreds of thousands of young black men in this country are not being prepared for a productive life is a national crisis. The statistics are almost unbelievable: a black boy born in 2001 has a one in three chance of going to prison. About 60 percent of black men who have dropped out spend some time in prison by the time they are in their mid-thirties. Other young men of color face similarly dismal statistics.

But statistics don't do justice to the truth of this catastrophe, because behind each dot we look at on a graph is, in truth, a heart-breaking story of a boy who could have done better. While is it useful to look at statistics to evaluate our progress or lack of progress, we must also remind ourselves constantly that we are looking at children with dreams and strengths and untapped skills. The boys in this book, by telling us their stories, remind us of the depths of their character that are overlooked by both statistics and popular culture.

Though many of these young authors have faced daunting challenges, they've found ways to make positive changes in their lives, and they share the hard-earned lessons they've learned. It can be lonely, and frightening, to leave the old ways behind in order to become more successful—whether that means letting go of friends who don't support your goals, or letting yourself be vulnerable enough to ask for help when you need it. By being honest about their struggles, and explicit about the things that helped them, these young men hope to show others what it takes to change.

I myself grew up in a poor, tough neighborhood, one of four boys raised by a single mother. I was a good student at school, but I was also good at learning the code of the streets. Thanks to a few lucky breaks I was able to follow my unspoken hopes of helping poor children like myself, eventually earning a graduate degree at the Harvard School of Education.

Many of the young men I grew up with had trouble finding good jobs, or got caught up in substance abuse. Some went to an early grave. But not all of us. The stories in this book are a vivid reminder that all boys are not the same. If we define them solely by their socio-economic status or their racial heritage, we are not really seeing them, which means that even well-meaning attempts at helping them will be hobbled. Each boy's path will be different and, if we are to empower them to find their way, we must provide a rich array of alternatives to the street.

We need to support young men as they navigate the difficult journey to adulthood, and walk the fine line between surviving on the block and succeeding outside of it. We need to show them that, like the boys in this book, they too have the power to take control of their own lives, to take advantage of educational opportunities, and to make meaningful choices about the kind of men they want to be. The Real Men program is a tool for educators and youth workers who want to empower young men to realize this potential within themselves.

And though young men may take different paths, the most important stop on every journey is a good education. To make sure that's possible, we need better public schools that are flexible enough to meet the needs of these boys. That will take a real revolution in how our schools function. And we need to address the myriad problems poor children face outside the classroom that can affect their performance inside the classroom. As important as math and English skills are, we have to think beyond our traditional school model. For example, research shows that the black-white achievement gap often starts at birth, so we need to ensure that young men who become parents learn the simple techniques to foster the kinds of brain development in their children that set the stage for school success. To really remove all of the barriers to learning, we need to make sure that children have good health care, that families in crisis get counseling, and that neighborhoods are made safe.

This can be done. Our birth-through-college pipeline in Harlem gets kids on track early, and we do whatever it takes to keep them on track for college and the high skills job market. As a society, we need to focus our political will to make that happen in many more places.

Who are these boys? They are our country's future and it is up to all of us to ensure that it is a bright future. Expanding comprehensive education programs like the Harlem Children's Zone, and using tools like the *Real Men* program, can help make that happen.

Who are these boys? They are ours.

Geoffrey Canada is CEO of the Harlem Children's Zone.

Table of Contents

Contents

WHERE WE ARE, AND WHERE WE WANT TO GO

2

Contents

STORIES TO ACCOMPANY *ALTERNATIVE HIGH*

Introduction

What makes a "real" man? A successful man? How do you become one? That's what the stories in this book are about.

The young men who wrote these stories know how hard it can be to figure out the answers. To become the men they wanted to be, they had to face a lot of other questions. Things like: How do you become a good father if you've never had one? How do you learn to trust if you've been betrayed by the people who should have been there for you? What does a loyal and loving relationship look like, and how do you build one? How do you manage the anger you feel? Is it OK to ask for help, and how do you get help that really works? Can you get respect in your neighborhood and still succeed outside of it?

These are big questions, and they can feel overwhelming. But these young men show how they've begun to find their own answers. They write about what has helped them, and the success they've had—using poetry or therapy to express pent-up emotions, persevering in spite of setbacks to find a job or finish high school or college, taking a risk to trust someone. Not everything they've tried has worked, and none of it was easy. But their stories show that if you're struggling with any of these questions and issues, you're not alone. You *can* figure it out, in a way that feels right for you. And there are a lot more possibilities than you might think.

Finally, by reading this book, you're not just doing yourself a favor. You're honoring the struggles of these writers as well. Each of them participated in Youth Communication's teen writing program. Some of these stories required more than 20 drafts and several months to write. At times, the writers will tell you, it felt like torture to continually reflect on their experiences, and to find the exact right words to convey what happened, how they felt, and what they learned from it. They subjected themselves to that process in part because it helped them get clarity on very important issues and struggles in their lives.

But for most of the writers, what really kept them going was knowing that if they could explain their struggles on paper, and show how they dealt with them, it would help someone else who was in a similar situation. They wrote these stories for you.

WHO WE ARE AND WHERE WE COME FROM

Chapter 1

People Who Shape Us

Deciding My Own Worth

By Juelz Long

1. I was 14, on my way to yet another foster home, with all my usual bad feelings roaming inside me. "What if I don't meet the family's standards?" I kept asking myself. "What are they going to say to me? What if I can't answer any of their questions?" I hated answering questions about myself because my answers were always negative.

As we got closer to my new home, I tried to imagine what the new family would be like. I was expecting a tired old foster mom like the ones I'd had in the past—the ones who just sat in the living room watching soap operas.

I went into foster care when I was 9 because my mother was too ill to take care of me. Since then I'd been in three foster homes. I felt like the reason people kept giving me up was because nobody liked me.

My first foster mom, Ms. Johnson (not her real name), was

always telling people how poorly I was doing in school, how lazy I was, and how I'd never amount to anything. She had terrible mood swings and yelled at me for everything. It was hard for me to function around her because I knew if I made a mistake, she'd yell.

2. **Nothing to Be Proud Of**

During my first summer with her, Ms. Johnson took me to my cousin's barbecue. I was excited because I hadn't been able to spend much time with my aunt and cousins since I'd gone into foster care. A friend of the family was downstairs waiting for us, and I rushed out of the house.

I don't remember what I did that ticked off Ms. Johnson, but when we got downstairs I ran in front of her to get to the car and she just went off.

> **I didn't want to participate in any family activities, like singing in the church choir, because I was afraid I'd embarrass myself.**

"Boy, I am so sick and tired of you. I want you out of my house, damn it!" she yelled so loudly that people looked out their windows. With everyone staring at me, I felt like we were on a movie set and I'd forgotten my lines. I just stood there quietly, too embarrassed and nervous to say anything.

I remember how the social worker would visit to see how things were going. When she'd ask me, "How's school?" my answer was always, "Not too good. I'm really disgusted with my performance in school and I know I could do better."

But I didn't know I could do better. I was just saying that because I was so used to Ms. Johnson saying it. She'd told me so often how disgusted she was with me that I'd become disgusted with myself. I felt my life was nothing to be proud of, nothing to talk about. My self-esteem was as low as it could be.

3. 'Daddy's Home'

Now here I was again, on my way to another new home. I'd been told I'd have two new foster sisters and a foster brother, so I was expecting a bad little 6- or 7-year-old who would get on my nerves. And I wasn't expecting a father at all, since I'd never had one in any of my previous foster homes. I figured the home would be quiet and boring like the ones I was used to. Boy, was I wrong.

My new foster mother greeted me at the door and I was surprised at how young she was—probably in her early 40s. And her biological son, Solomon, was two years older than me. He showed me my new room, which was cool, with posters, a computer, and a video game system.

He told me a little about the house rules and chores, and I began to feel more relaxed. It was the first time I actually felt comfortable coming into a new foster home. Then Solomon looked out the window and said, "Daddy's home."

I felt my heart stop for a minute. I took a huge breath and tried to remain calm. I was scared that I wouldn't make a good impression. I didn't want him to think I was a big screw-up.

But when Mr. Long came upstairs, he just looked in the room and said, "Hello." He looked like a young, built guy. But he was more calm than scary. He didn't bother me, ask me questions, or give me a huge lecture about the rules of the house. He just walked into his room and started watching TV.

4. Hard to Believe

My new foster family made me feel like I was part of the family from the day I arrived. They joked around with me, let me talk on the phone or make myself something to eat. The parents told me to call them Mom and Dad instead of Mrs. and Mr. Long. And whenever someone asked them who I was, they'd say "my son" or "my brother."

Even so, for a while I pretty much stayed to myself. I still didn't believe I could hold a mature conversation, or any conversation at all. I didn't want to participate in any family activities, like singing in the church choir, because I was afraid I'd embarrass myself. Not because I thought I would make a mistake, but because I thought I *was* a mistake.

My new foster parents constantly told me I was smart, that I was just as good as anyone else and I could be anything I wanted to be. They said that as long as I tried my best, I would get the best in return. I wanted to believe them, but after being told I was worthless for so long, it was hard.

5. **The Lawn Mower**

One day, a few weeks after I arrived, my father told me to go outside and mow the front lawn. I couldn't believe this man actually trusted me to cut his beautiful grass, and I was terrified.

Solomon showed me how to turn the lawn mower on and off, and the rest was up to me. I started mowing, but stopped every two minutes because I really thought I was going to mess up. It took me about an hour to finish, and when I was done, it looked a little uneven. I felt I could've done better.

> **I was still waiting for those five words I'd heard all my life: "You could have done better."**

Even though it was my first time mowing a lawn, I didn't bother to reward myself with a pat on the back. I was just disappointed, because that was my natural response to everything I did.

I could feel the blood rushing through my body as I walked toward my dad's bedroom to tell him I'd finished. He went outside to take a look, and five minutes passed before he came back inside. I heard the door close and he told me to come downstairs.

"Oh, here we go," I said to myself. I knew he was going to tell me I'd done a bad job. When I got to the last step, I was so nervous I felt like I was standing in front of millions of people.

6. Waiting for Those Words

"Pass me my bag," he said. I noticed he didn't look angry at all. But I was still waiting for him to say those five words I'd heard all my life: "You could have done better."

I gave him his bag without taking my eyes off him. Finally I couldn't wait anymore. "That was my first time cutting grass. I know I could've done much better," I said.

Then he said something that I'd never heard before. "Well, I think you did a wonderful job. It looks real nice." He took $20 out of his bag and handed it to me.

My dad didn't seem at all surprised by my success with the lawn. That's when I realized he'd already known I could do it. He believed in me.

It took somebody else's confidence in me to help me gain confidence in myself. All my life I'd accepted what people said and thought about me. Not for a second had I thought to myself, "You know what? I'm going to prove them all wrong."

> **It took somebody else's confidence in me to help me gain confidence in myself.**

7. An Unforgettable Present

Now I felt like a different person, because I had different people around me. I finally had a brother I could bond with about guy things like cars and girls. I had a younger sister I could look out for and an older sister at Yale University.

I had a father who was an elementary school principal and a leader in his church. He could show me the way to manhood, teaching me how to do things like mow the lawn and paint the house so one day I'd be able to take care of my own family.

And I had a mother I could talk to. She's a junior high school guidance counselor, and when times got hard or stressful for me, she was easy to confide in.

My new family fell in love with me and vice versa. Before long, I decided I wanted to make things permanent. I wanted to be adopted. It took a few years to get through all the paperwork, but a week before my 17th birthday I was finally officially adopted. That was a birthday present I'll never forget.

I've been with my family for three years now, and they're like my special basketball team. In basketball, the player holding the ball has teammates to help him score the basket. My parents and siblings are my teammates and I know they'll stand behind me all the way, helping me to achieve my goals, reminding me that I can do it, that I'm worth something.

8. A Speech to the Congregation

Sometimes I do still find myself caught up in my emotions and asking myself, "Do I really belong here? Am I comfortable? Did I really want to be adopted?" It's like I'm unsure whether I can make it last. I'm still working on getting that father and son connection I've never had before. There's so much to learn about being part of a family, and sometimes I'm afraid I can't learn it all.

> **Now I felt like a different person, because I had different people around me.**

But I guess that's what being a family is all about — ups and downs. And when I remember all the things I went through before I met my family, the things they've done to show me the light at the end of the tunnel mean even more to me.

About a month ago, it was Youth Day at my church and my mother, who's the youth president, had all the kids do an assignment. We had to take something you'd find in a building, like windows or an elevator, and explain it spiritually to the congregation.

I chose the incinerator, which was kind of scary because nothing in the Bible refers to an incinerator. But when it was time for me to give my speech, I was ready.

9. **The Incinerator**

"Now we'll have 'Incinerator,' by brother Joey," my mother said. I got up and all eyes were on me. I was nervous, as usual, but for some reason I knew I had everything under control.

"That boy don't even have it written on paper! Go ahead Joe!" my father yelled out from the congregation. By the time I got to the front I had a smile on my face.

"The incinerator," I said. "This is like a dumpsite or trash can, correct?"

"Amen," replied a lady in the congregation.

"And what do we do with garbage?" I asked.

"Put it in the incinerator!" the congregation shouted back.

"You see, church," I continued, gaining more confidence as I preached on, "the garbage can be anything. It can be the stress in your life. It can be the words of people who badmouth you behind your back. What do we call those people?"

"Phonies!" the congregation replied.

With my father and now the whole church rooting me on, I figured out what it was I wanted to say. "Phonies put out negativity that we don't want around us," I said. "They only put obstacles in our way. It's up to us to say, 'I don't need that negative stuff in my life. I'm going to get rid of it and start over.' So, in reference to the incinerator, when you have garbage, get rid of it."

10. **Choosing What to Keep**

After I finished, many congregants made comments like, "That was beautiful," and "We have Reverend Joey in the house." I held my hand on my chest, took a deep breath and thought, "Wow, I can't believe I did it." I'd never before let people see the bright side of me. I always got too scared, so I never accomplished anything.

That day was the start of movement for me. It made me realize that I'm smart, creative, and just as good as anybody else.

I think the reason the words came to me so easily when I was giving my speech is because it was symbolic of what's happened in my own life. For most of my life I allowed outside forces to destroy my self-image.

Now I've thrown those negative forces away, like garbage. Instead, I'm taking what's useful and positive from outside myself, like the encouragement of my family, to create my own positive self-image.

Juelz was 17 when he wrote this story.

Step-Family Ties

By Jordan Temple

1. I wasn't with my mother last Thanksgiving. I wasn't with my father, either. I spent the holiday with my father's ex-wife Dawn and her family. I've been close to them ever since my dad married Dawn about 10 years ago.

I still call Dawn my mother because she takes care of me and gives me good advice. She's stern but understanding, and is the mother of my little brother, Joshua, 8, and sister, Tara, 10, whom I love very much. She encourages my relationship with them and keeps me up-to-date on Joshua's drum recitals and Tara's piano lessons. When I visit, about once a month, we watch TV together, run around, and play board games.

I was 7 or 8 when I first met Dawn. She and my father would pick me up from my mom's house for weekend visits. Luckily, my mother and stepmother got along and pretty much saw eye-to-eye on parenting. They'd talk on the phone about me, Tara, and Joshua. My mother would send me over to their house with a gift for my stepmother during the holidays and vice versa.

2. **Three of Everything**

I never thought about it until recently, but it's refreshing that everyone was cool with each other. My mother had met my step-grandparents, and my stepmother knew my mother's mother.

I recently found out that my mom sometimes got sad when I left home to see my dad and stepmom. She said I looked like my stepmother and father's child when I was with them, and people often mistook me for Dawn's son. But my mom never seemed upset or jealous around me. And I liked having three families (my mother's side, my father's side, and my stepmother's side) because it was like I had three of almost everything. I had plenty of aunts and cousins.

> I like having the perspective of more than one "mom."

I have a good relationship with my mom and I appreciate all the time and energy she sacrificed to raise me as a single parent after she and my dad broke up. But it was good having Dawn as another person in my corner. Just like with her own children, Dawn wanted to see me succeed. She also understood me a lot better than my father because she's younger, and her job is working with students at a college. She's always been a good influence on me.

One of the greatest memories I have of my stepmother is when she let me hold my baby sister, Tara, for the first time. Tara was such a remarkable thing to me. I'd never had a sister, and never held such a little baby (just a week old). I fed her, changed her, and burped her. It was wild. I knew that my stepmother had to trust me to let me do all this, and that was very special to me.

3. **Someone I Can Talk To**

The relationship between my stepmother and father broke down after 10 years. I could see them disagreeing on things. My father worked so much and so hard, it seemed they had no time to work out their differences. My stepmother told my brother, sister, and me about the divorce at the same time. My father moved out and they sold the house.

But I never thought my relationship with my stepmother would change, and it didn't. After a couple of months, I called her and went to visit with her and the kids again.

I could talk to her, and I think I got along with her better than I could with my father. He sometimes asked me if I was still speaking to Dawn, but he didn't seem upset to hear that I was. I liked knowing that Dawn and her entire side of the family wanted me to come over on weekends as much as I wanted to see them.

To this day, Dawn talks to me about issues I may have in my neighborhood or school, and about current events. She's always told me the basic parents' rhetoric: that education is important, to study, and also to listen to my (birth) mother. My mother talks to me about these things, too, but I like having the perspective of more than one "mom."

4. **A Family Thanksgiving**

I go to my stepmother's house once every month or two, but last November was my first Thanksgiving there. When I got to the house, my step-grandma and step-grandpa greeted me with open arms. I could see that my brother and sister had missed me a lot. They played video games with their cousin, while everyone else made turkey, macaroni and cheese, and cornbread. I helped put together the lasagna.

The tablecloth was laid out and an extra leaf was put into the serving table. By the time my step-aunt brought in the eggnog ice cream, I was already rubbing my stomach. It felt like a very regular, irregular Thanksgiving. I could taste happiness as I munched on a turkey leg.

It felt good to pack up my bags and be somewhere besides my house for the holidays for a change. I watched football, and saw my Jets' season go even further down the tubes. The Jets lost 34-3, but hanging out with my family, I felt like a winner. My step-family is just as important to me as my immediate family because I know that even though I don't see them as much, they care about me just the same. Their good wishes for me to do well in college mean as much to me as my blood family's wishes, and that is truly something that I am thankful for.

It was also pretty cool to have two sets of Thanksgiving leftovers. Neither tasted better than the other, because I loved them both.

Jordan was 20 when he wrote this story.

My Father: I Want to Be Everything He's Not

By Troy Shawn Welcome

1. **M**y father was very popular in Guyana, South America, where we lived until I was 9 years old. His friends used to tell me how it was difficult to walk down the street with him without being noticed. I could only wonder about that because I never spent time with my father. I saw him only on those rare occasions when he slept at home.

My father was what you'd call a playboy. He had a son with one of his mistresses and also a daughter with a second mistress.

But despite all of his faults, I still admired my father. When his friends heard me speak, laugh, or walk, they'd say, "That's Terry's son alright." I was just like my dad, and I felt proud to be like him. He was my role model.

After we moved to America, he and my mother started to fight constantly. I hated when they fought, because he'd hit her.

He started disappearing for days and then weeks at a time. For some time I'd only see him on weekends. One weekend, he took my brother and me to a Yankee game. I don't like baseball; the only thing I liked about the game was that he was there.

But the thing I remember the most was the weekend when he taught my brother Rob and me how to ride bicycles at the track and field next to Yankee Stadium. I remember going down the straightaway part of the track with my pops at my side. I felt a bond with him.

2. **Weekends Together**

Those weekends were great, but they didn't last. When I was 11, I started to see him less and less each month. I'd wake up on Saturday mornings hoping to see him that day, but most of the time I'd be disappointed. After about a year he called and asked Rob and me to spend weekends with him in New Jersey, where he was now living. Even though I was happy to be with him, I didn't show it that much. I was hurt because he had left us for so long.

> **Those weekends with my dad were great, but they didn't last.**

The weekend stays at his house went so well that he asked us to spend the summer with him. I enjoyed that summer. He'd leave money on my pillow before he left for work in the morning. I looked forward to hearing his van pull up when he came home. I felt mad good because I had a dad again.

3. **Wedding Bells**

The year that followed was good because I saw him almost every weekend. Then one day my father picked up my brother and me and took us shopping. He bought us suits, shirts, and ties, and we went to his house in New Jersey, where he was living with a woman named Fay.

The house smelled like a bakery and there were a lot of suits lying on the couch. I had no idea what was going on, so I joined two of Fay's sons who were playing video games.

Suddenly my pops came into the living room, called me and my brother over into the corner, put his arms around us, and said, "We're going to a wedding on Saturday."

"Whose wedding?" I asked.

"Me and Fay's," he answered.

I had an idea that he'd say that. I was happy for him. I rejoined Fay's sons at the television, hoping to start a conversation because I really felt like I didn't belong. "Yo, you heard... your moms and my pops are getting married," I said.

"We knew that for a year already. You just found out?" Shawn asked.

I was embarrassed because my brother and I were the only people who hadn't known. I thought that everyone was laughing at me. "Now he has new sons and he doesn't need me anymore," I thought.

4. **Treated Like a Stepchild**

On the morning of the wedding, my brother and I had to help decorate the hall where the ceremony and reception were to be held. It was hard work, but hours later the hall was transformed with tablecloths and all kinds of decorations. I didn't mind doing all that work because I was looking forward to being a part of the wedding.

But I didn't have anything to do with the ceremony. When it was over, I was still hoping to sit with my father, but I could have waited years for him to notice me. I was disappointed and upset. I felt as though my pops used me as his maid, as though I wasn't important to him.

After the wedding I spoke to my father only when it was absolutely necessary. As years raced by, the number of times that I saw him decreased.

I was angry at my pops for treating me like a stepchild at the wedding, but I still needed him in my life. It was very hard, and still is, to be a teen and my own father at the same time. I'd question whether I was good enough to be considered a man. I couldn't get through a day without stressing myself out about whether I acted, talked, or looked like a man. All that stress affected my life in many ways.

5. **The Confrontation**

Finally, about a year and a half ago, after years of keeping my feelings inside and many, many sessions with my counselor, I raised the courage to call my father up and confront him.

"What kind of father are you?" I asked him. "You don't call, you don't come to see us. If anyone met me in the last two years, they'd think that I didn't have a father. I don't understand what's going on."

"Ah, um, I have been calling and coming by," he countered calmly. "But you are never there."

The way he spoke to me made me feel like we were two executives at a board meeting.

"You haven't been calling or coming cause I would've gotten a message," I said. "I think it's because you got your new sons and Karen [my older half-sister] over there, so you don't need us anymore."

> **I couldn't get through a day without stressing myself out about whether I acted, talked, or looked like a man.**

I was hoping that he'd say that it wasn't true and that he still loved me, but that didn't happen.

"I don't think you should be taking this tone with me," he said. He was starting to get upset. "You call me up and tell me this bull about—"

"Bull?" I interrupted. "This ain't bull. It's the way I feel. I'm telling you the way I feel and that's all it is to you—bull crap!"

"OK, it's the way you feel. But I'm still your father and you shouldn't be speaking to me like this," he said.

"As far as I'm concerned, you're not my father. You haven't

been and will never be my father," I told him.

"You will always be my son and we will be together in the future," he said in a patronizing voice.

"If you're not here for me now, what makes you think that I'm going to need you in the future?" I said. "Listen, I have another call so I gotta go, a'ight."

Click.

The conversation pissed me off. First, he had an annoying tone throughout the conversation. It made me feel like he wasn't taking me seriously. Second, he made me realize that I was right—he didn't want me.

But I felt a little relieved to at least know how he felt. It was the hardest thing that I ever did. I was trembling while I was speaking to him. My emotions were so strong from keeping them in for so many years. It was good for me to get them out because now I don't think about him enough to get me depressed anymore.

> **Finally, I raised the courage to call my father up and confront him.**

6. **The Last Straw**

Surprisingly, he did call me back a few weeks later. He told me that he wanted to hang out with my brother and me that Friday. I canceled my plans just so I could be with my dad.

At 7 o'clock on Friday night I was waiting for him. Nine o'clock came and I was getting frustrated because I hate waiting for people. I finally decided to call and find out if something happened to him. Fay answered the phone and told me he was sleeping. She woke him up and he gave me some story about having a long day. Then he asked if he could see me on Sunday and I agreed.

To make a long story short, he never came on Sunday. From that day I realized that I was never going to have him in my life again. I haven't seen or heard from my sperm donor (that's what

I call him sometimes) since that conversation—a year and a half ago.

7. **Mom Says I Should Love Him**

My mother still tries to convince me that I should love him because he's my father. But how can I love someone I don't know and who doesn't know me?

Today things are better. I've managed to hide my feelings for my father so deep that I'd have to dig to find them. I still think he doesn't want me. But I realize that no matter what he did to me, it's no excuse for me to have a messed-up life.

Strangely enough, he did teach me something. He taught me that the best man I could be is his total opposite. I now know that having children left and right doesn't make a man. Staying around to raise them does.

Troy was 19 when he wrote this story. His relationship with his dad continued to affect him (read more about it in p. 212).

Back in Touch

By Eric Benson

1. I felt extremely bad about myself as a parent when I came to prison. As a teenager I had really wanted a son. Once he was finally born, I was arrested and left him. Now, 14 years later, I still regret every day that I am not the parent that my son needed.

   I have a few good memories of my son. When I held him he would stop crying. I loved the way he drooled when I took his bottle out of his mouth. I also remember taking him to a carnival in Virginia, not long before I got locked up.

2. **Paying the Price**

   I was arrested when I was 20 and my son was just 4 months old. I left him home with his mother that day. I pulled out of the driveway with two friends in the car and drove for just half a block when a police car came toward me, head on. There were police in the car behind me, too.

When I stopped, they jumped out with their guns drawn. I pictured my son's face at that moment. I had a really bad feeling. I knew that my past was about to catch up with me.

I was sent to prison in February 1993. Soon his mother and I broke up, and she decided that it was best that my son and I not have a relationship while I was in prison. I begged to differ. I stayed persistent year after year, writing to her, attempting to establish a relationship with my son.

I never would've imagined that our separation would last for more than 14 years.

3. **Determined to Mature**

In prison I began to transform my life. I looked at my past mistakes and told myself that I was going to mature into a man and a responsible father. I dedicated myself to becoming educated and growing up so that, when given the opportunity, I could be the parent that my son deserved.

> **I dedicated myself to becoming educated and growing up, so I could be the parent that my son deserved.**

Other prisoners often tell me that I have been handling my situation the right way. Their words of encouragement help me to persevere.

At last, my persistence in trying to communicate with my son paid off. Not long ago, my son's mother finally allowed him to come visit me. It was the first time since he was an infant that I'd ever held or hugged my son.

4. **'Shocked to See You'**

That first visit was like an out-of-body experience. I was at work and the correctional officer called me and said, "You have a first-time visitor. Do you want to go on the visit?" He didn't tell me who it was, and I was curious to know who might be coming to see me for the first time when I'd been locked up for more than

14 years. "Of course I want my visit," I said.

In the visiting room, the officer told me, "Your visitors are in Row 4, Table 6." I didn't recognize the first man at the table, my son's uncle.

Then I saw my son sitting with his head down on the table. Somehow, I recognized him immediately. My son is 6' 2" and has short hair like me. His bone structure is so similar to mine. He has big dark brown eyes and a familiar blush. Our baby pictures look just alike.

5. Happy and Stunned

I was extremely happy and stunned, but I still found the voice to say, "How's everything with you, Kharon?"

"I'm OK," he said.

I asked him, "Can I have a hug?" He gave me a hug and we sat down.

"Kharon, how are you feeling right now?" I asked.

"Shocked to see you," he said.

I told him, "Everything is going to be all right."

I had so much I wanted to tell him. I started from the beginning, from when I left him as a baby. Time wouldn't allow me to express everything that I wanted to say on that day, however. When I returned to my cell I wrote him a long letter to say more about things we hadn't had time to talk about.

6. Us Time, Finally

I stayed up for most of that night thinking about our visit and how my son looked so much like me. I cried tears of joy for finally being able to look my son in the face and hug him after so long. My heart was swollen with happiness.

On our second visit, we were communicating like close friends. I was surprised that he seemed to talk to me about any and everything. He didn't hold back.

He even talked to me about girls—I couldn't believe that! He also asked me where he'd gotten his height from, because he's taller than both his mother and me. I couldn't really answer that. Then he said, "You look just like me!" I said, "No, you look like me."

I asked him to write all of his questions down. His letter made me so happy. He had quite a few questions for me, like: "What is your favorite color? What sports did you like to play when you were younger? Were you ever an 'A' student in school? Were you ever a ladies' man?" That last question threw me for a loop.

He said he didn't want to OD with the questions, but I didn't mind. I'd been waiting for the opportunity to communicate and establish a relationship with my son. I was happy to see him opening up to me in such a short time.

7. Too Much Like Me?

Since our first visit, I've been able to see my son once a month through the Osborne Association, an organization that helps incarcerated parents and their children. I'm feeling really good about how Kharon and I are getting to know each other. I can see us building a beautiful father-and-son relationship.

> **I also worry about my son. I see how he holds the same materialistic mindset that I had as a teenager.**

But I also worry about my son. I see how he holds the same materialistic mindset that I had as a teenager. That mindset hurt me in my life, and I am scared of the influence the streets can have on a materialistic 15-year-old. Will it affect my son as negatively as it affected me?

Going to parenting class helped. I learned about teenagers' typical behaviors, and I hope what I learned will help me steer my son the right way as I get to know him better. I talk to my son a lot about growing up and taking on the responsibilities of adulthood, and about being able to respect himself first before thinking about others respecting him. I want him to understand that the decisions that he makes now will affect his future.

8. The Happiest Father

At the end of the parenting class, I was privileged to have my son at my graduation. I gave a speech about my quest to establish a relationship with him. I was the happiest father on the planet that day. When I finished my speech, Kharon came up to the podium and gave me the biggest hug a son could give his father.

It has been more than nine months since my son and I got back in contact. I hope and pray that all goes well with my son while I continue my journey in prison, due to the bad decisions that I made when I was not much older than Kharon is now.

Eric wrote this story for Rise, *a magazine by and for parents. Reprinted with permission. www.risemagazine.org.*

My Father, My Friend

By Macario DeLaCruz

1.   It's said that everybody has a double in the world who they'll probably never meet. Well, I've met mine; I've known him all my life. No, he's not my twin, but he is my reflection.

Or maybe I'm his. I'm speaking about my father—the lighter, older, and shorter version of me. Or am I the darker, younger, and taller version of him? When I let my hair grow, even though it's curlier than his, I look just like he did at my age.

Our temperaments and personalities are similar, too. We're both laid-back, realistic, and good-natured guys. We don't get angry much, though we do get annoyed quickly. When we're thinking deeply we both rub our thumb and pointer finger across our bottom lip and fold our hands in front of our face the same way. And we can both wiggle our ears.

He's just like me. It's weird, yet cool—I think.

2. **Hanging in Manhattan**

I don't live with my dad; my parents separated when I was 6 or 7. I live with my mother and brother in Brooklyn, New York. But I see my dad, who lives by himself in Manhattan, often.

My parents generally get along fine; they just can't live with one another. My dad visits us in Brooklyn whether my mom is home or not.

But most of the time I see him when I go to Manhattan and hook up with him there. Usually it's just to get a bite to eat, but sometimes we'll go to the movies or shopping for games, books, DVDs, or clothes. And I can call him any time.

Even though we don't live together (or maybe because we don't), we're very close. I can talk to him about everything—sports, video games, politics, music, life, rain, computers (even though he doesn't know much about them), writing, yoga, fish, or anything. No topic is taboo.

I admire my dad a lot as well. If I had to describe him with one word, it would be: sage. He's highly intelligent and wise.

Like the prophet lady from *The Matrix*, he tells you what you need to hear. The general theme of his advice is: "Put the work in if you want to get anything out of it and accomplish things in life."

3. **People See Us as Friends**

People who see us together often think we're friends and not father and son. The other day, my dad and I were shopping and he bought some shoes. As the cashier rang them up, she and my dad asked each other about their ethnic backgrounds. He told her he was black and Filipino. She said she was American, because she was born here, but she's also Chinese, because her parents were born there.

Then she asked, "What about your friend?" referring to me, of course. He said laughingly, "That's my son."

She replied, "Yeah, OK," like she didn't believe him.

After showing her our IDs (and our same names, Macario

DeLaCruz), she remarked that she was astonished by how young my dad looked, and how we looked like friends, or maybe brothers, but not father and son.

When we left the store I jokingly told him, as I often do, "If it wasn't for me, you wouldn't have those good looks, you know." He laughed and smiled, then we grabbed a bite to eat.

4. **Young for a Dad**

I'm not sure why people peg my father and me as friends and not brothers. I think it's probably because even though I think we look alike, I'm much darker than him, my hair isn't like his (mine's curly and long, while his is straight and short) and my frame is bigger than his.

Our relationship is totally different from my friends' and their dads. For one thing, my dad is pretty young. All of my friends' dads are in their 40s, while my dad is 36.

(My mom is young, too. Occasionally, people think we're friends, but 90% of the time they think we're brother and sister.)

5. **We Agree on Tupac**

My dad and I also share the same interests, like video games and music. We both like rap, r&b, and hip-hop, and consider Tupac Shakur the greatest rapper of all time. We're also both into Jimi Hendrix and Lenny Kravitz, and though my dad's not a big rock fan, he loves some of the same rock albums I do.

I know for a fact that my friends' fathers have no interest in listening to rap and haven't the remotest interest in playing video games. Their only concern about video games is how much it's going to cost them to buy their kid's next system.

But there are some things about my dad I just don't get, like his passion for Starbucks. Every day, at least twice, he has to have a big ol' cup of his favorite coffee, Iced Grande Americano. To me, iced coffee defeats the purpose of coffee by being cold. To make matters worse, my dad doesn't add milk, but adds enough sugar to cause the coffee to overflow.

While I shudder at the thought of cold coffee, I drink coffee too. But I can't see ever participating in my dad's hideous habit of smoking cigarettes. To give him credit, he's started to cut down, or he says he has. And at least he doesn't smell like smoke. I've told him to quit, but I haven't pushed him. If he decides to quit, then I'll be happy.

6. My 'Old Man' Does Yoga

It's weird that my dad smokes, which has a terrible effect on your lungs, but also does yoga, which helps a person's breathing. As he's always telling me, "Yoga will teach you how to breathe correctly and it will help you focus." I think he's intent on doing yoga to counteract his smoking habit.

He's tried to get me into yoga, but I'm not very interested. I'll stick to basketball and football and sometimes baseball, but I'll leave yoga for the "old man." It seems more for older people and people who are stressed out, like college students.

As I've gotten older, my dad and I have slowly gotten closer. When we go our separate ways, there's no kiss on the cheek or just a plain ol' "Goodbye," like how some of my friends say bye to their fathers. Instead, we give each other a pound.

That may seem odd to people who are used to seeing only friends doing that with friends, but to me and my dad, it's second nature, an unconscious action. I wouldn't have it any other way.

Macario was 17 when he wrote this story.
He graduated from high school and went to college.

My Street Brothers

By Derrick B.

1. I think I was born to travel, cause I have been doing so my whole life. No one ever had the time to think about what I wanted or how I was feeling. I'm 18 now and I grew up without a father and without a loving mother in my life. If it were not for all the other family members I grew up with, I would never have made it.

When I talk about other family members, I don't mean blood relatives. I'm talking about the people everyone has that they go to for help with a problem or to learn something new in life. I'm talking about the family that's always there when you need to share a secret, or always has a joke to tell when your day is going rough. I'm talking about friends.

It was not until I was 13 that my mind and body rebelled against the abuse in my life. I wanted better for myself and I realized being good at home or school would not make my family proud of me, cause they never had time to notice. So I decided to find a new family and forget about everybody else.

2. **A True Hustler**

Back then, I was very, very shy and I only had one friend, CJ. He was like a brother to me. The only difference between us was that I was a good boy and he was bad.

CJ was a hustler. He was only one year older than me but I thought he had something I would die for—he seemed happy with his life. He had bricks of money in his pocket, a nice phone, good clothes, and a fine-looking girlfriend.

I met CJ one day when I was walking through the park and noticed his girl. I didn't know she had a man at the time so my instinct told me to smile and wave. The first thing he did was argue with his girl and quickly walk towards me. I'm thinking I'm about to get beat up for looking at a girl. He came close and looked me in the eyes

"You need something?" he asked.

3. **Finding a Friend**

"Oh no, no, I was just smiling at your beautiful girlfriend. I thought she was alone," I said. I was trying to talk like I was tough enough to be a gangster, so he wouldn't think about fighting. CJ smiled.

"Yeah I know man, you ain't got to explain yourself. I mean she do look good. But I was asking if you need something else." Right then I knew he was not only cool but a hustler as well.

"Nah, I don't use drugs," I said, trying to speak soft so I wouldn't blow his cover. He smiled when I spoke low and asked if I still wanted to chill and meet his girl.

We spent the rest of the day in the park, and as time went by CJ and I hung out all over New York. We would go to the movies and eat at restaurants.

CJ would pull out hundreds of dollars and spend it like water. I knew he got the money from the drugs he sold, and I did not want to ask him about it. My life was bad but I was taught drugs could kill you. But I was starting to realize that keeping pain bottled up inside could kill me too.

4. **Taking the Green Stuff**

I had never opened up to anyone about how my mother beat me. Not since I told my teachers one day and got another beating for telling. But one day, a few months after I met him, CJ just made me feel like I could trust him with anything.

It was after a particularly loud fight with my mom. I stormed out of the house trying to escape the fury in my heart. I could never understand her ways and running was the only way I could win a war with her. I ran all the way to the park and I sat down on a bench and cried. That's when CJ spotted me.

> **I felt like I was on a natural high that only went away if I calmed down.**

"Yo, Derrick, what happened?" he said, standing with his girl beside him. I wasn't going to explain until I saw his fist ball up. Right there I felt I could trust him. He was already on my side, ready to defend my back. I told him everything that happened and he and Jasmine just listened as they started to put some green stuff inside a split cigar.

After I finished my story, I noticed a tear in Jasmine's eye. I looked down and finally asked about the cigar. "What's that?" I asked.

CJ looked at me and smiled. "This is going to help you forget your problems at home and make you happy again," he said.

"So what is it?" I asked before I took a pull.

"It's called weed," Jasmine said, and smiled.

5. **Blunting the Pain**

After that first pull off the blunt, I became a different child. Instead of getting in trouble at home I chilled on the streets with CJ and got in bigger trouble.

I started smoking a lot and opening myself up to people instead of being the quiet kid. CJ would invite me to his house and he would introduce me to his friends. I realized every time I met a new friend, I'd be smoking with them. It seemed like the popular kids would never notice you unless you did drugs and shared it with everybody, or you were a wild kid who knew how to hustle and get money to spend on everybody. In time, I did both.

> **Those guys helped me feel better, like I wasn't alone. But they never helped me move my life in a safe direction.**

As time flew by, I became known to a lot of people on the streets. I was not really a popular kid but the people I hung out with had grown to have a lot of respect for me. I still had problems at home with my mom and she would still hit me for reasons I never understood. But a few months of meeting new friends and smoking weed every day made me not care what she did to me.

One time she was beating me while I was high. Instead of crying and crawling for safety under my bed or inside my closet I ran around the house laughing at her cause she couldn't catch me. I was happy about the way my life was starting to change, now that I had plenty of friends to chill with whenever I didn't want to be at home.

6. **I Wasn't Alone**

Then my mom put me in foster care, and I was sent to a group home. At first I could not get over the fact that my mother just abandoned me. I was upset not only with her but the world. Now I had to start my life over with no family or a true best friend to talk to. I was worried about how I would be treated in a group home.

I was placed in a house with guys who were older than me, but to my surprise they took me in. The guys made me feel like

I wasn't alone. On my 14th birthday, I got drunk for the first time with one of my new friends, a guy named Manny. Manny made me forget about my mom and my problems. He gave me one thing I'd always wanted from my mom: attention.

Now, Manny was a real smart hustler. He taught me how to make money selling the weed I always smoked. I never knew I could do that.

Two months later I had to move to another group home. I was upset because yet again I had built a bond with someone only to have it snatched away from me. But I would never forget all the things Manny and I did together that helped me learn how to adapt. I learned while I was around him to not worry about all the bad things that I'd been through. I started to think, when you've got money and your own way of making yourself happy, why should anything else bother you?

7. How to Forget

I made friends like Manny in each of the seven group homes I lived in. If it were not for all those friends, I don't think I would have made it. They all taught me that bad things happen to everyone. It's just up to me how I deal with the problem until I can finally let it go.

One way my friends would forget their problems was by causing new ones. At first I did not understand this because I thought more problems would build more stress. The type of problems my friends got into led to more trouble. But for some strange reason, trouble was kind of helpful when I thought about my life too much.

Whenever I did dumb things that my friends put me up to, I always had to get myself out of the problem alone. I always felt uncomfortable doing each stunt. But I also wanted to fit in with my friends, and I enjoyed the excitement of trying to escape the police.

I robbed people in the parks and stole phones from stores. The excitement of running from the law blocked out all my problems. I felt like I was on a natural high that only went away if I calmed down, and I did not want to calm down.

When I did get away with crimes on my own, the guys would praise me and give me pats on the back. Next thing I knew, people I'd never seen before knew my name. I was famous and I had a few girls who also liked the wild side of me. I was blind to the negative effects of what I was doing.

8. Waking Up

But recently I met Kyanni, the first girl I actually fell in love with. Really caring for someone, and having her genuinely care about me, started to change my perspective. She helped me wake up to the fact that I've only got three more years until I age out of foster care and have to be independent.

At that time, I will be old enough to have a place of my own and not worry about moving unless I want to. But for the past five years, I have not been working legally and I don't have any money or a bank account. All I did every day was smoke my brains away, drop out of school, and get in trouble with the people I called friends.

At first, when those guys were around and telling me their life stories, they helped me feel better, like I wasn't alone. I realized I wasn't the only one who'd been let down by his family. They taught me how to look after myself on the streets.

> **Lately, I've realized I want the type of friends who encourage me to be successful.**

But as I think about it now, they never gave me any advice that helped me move my life in a safe direction for the future, the way Kyanni did. They taught me that, instead of worrying about the past or the future, I should focus on the excitement of the day I woke up to.

Lately, I've realized I want the type of friends who don't just help you forget the past or survive the present, but give you advice and encouragement on being successful in the future.

9. What Are Friends For?

When the people I thought were my friends heard I only had a short time to get my life together before I'd be forced to live on the streets, they did not even act concerned. They only cared about when I was going to support their next high.

Still, I can't say I regret the time I spent with them. My friends taught me the things I needed to survive at the time. They were my street brothers and sisters, and they helped me get by. But now it's time to move on.

Derrick was 18 when he wrote this story.

Chapter 2

Places That Shape Us

Hear No Evil, See No Evil...
Do No Evil

By Curtis Holmes

1. When I was younger, I was pretty upset that my parents gave me so many responsibilities and had so many rules, and that I had to come home right after school every day and babysit my little sister.

But when I watched the friend I once looked up to as a brother fall into trouble, it made me think that maybe my responsibilities were a blessing in disguise. In some ways it made me be even more strict with myself than my parents were with me. I mean, if he could go to church for years and still get lured into street life, couldn't that happen to me?

I am not making any excuses for him—he was lured, not pushed. But if you had asked me before, I would never have expected my friend to get in trouble like that. He's smart and has a mother who cares about him no matter what he does. But I guess that wasn't enough. He started off small, just cutting classes and getting a few suspensions, but he ended up getting in trouble with the police and finally landed in jail.

2. It's So Easy to Mess Up

So who is to say what could happen? There are hundreds of stories about people with so much promise who have failed, which is why I put the pressure on myself to succeed and not mess up.

The way I live my life every day is far different than how other people around my way live theirs. I come home, take care of my homework, study, read, and watch my sister. I watch TV and sometimes I go outside. But I don't hang out too much with the kids in my neighborhood, and I don't go to parties or stay out late.

> **Maybe my responsibilities were a blessing in disguise.**

You'll never see me drinking or smoking. Besides school and sleep, church takes up most of the rest of my week. There are services on Tuesday, Thursday, and Sunday. And every month there are youth meetings where I have most of my friends.

And one thing I never do is treat a challenge as unimportant, no matter what it is.

3. I've Got Blinders On

If you ever see horses at a race track, you'll see that they wear blinders on the sides of their eyes. That's so that they can't look to their right or left to see what anyone else is doing. I am like those horses. I don't look to my left and see the drugs and alcohol. I will not look to my right and see the sex. I will only look ahead to finish the race.

Sometimes the blinders do prevent me from doing things that other people do. Sometimes I feel I am living a life where I'm stuck with my little sister after school, cooking and cleaning like a maid. Sometimes I want to party all night, do all the things I just said I will never do.

I want to be the big willie who has everybody wanting to be like him. Also, though I have some good friends who I've had for a while, I don't make that many new friends and I don't have a girlfriend.

You can ask my friend Michelle. She'll tell you that most of the time when I am alone and looking sad, it's not because something is wrong, it is just that I am not used to being with people a lot, which makes me anti-social.

4. **Sacrificing for the Future**

I know that by living this lifestyle I might miss out on some interesting experiences and people in the short term, but that is something that I can live with. I just tell myself that anything I can do with a girl now for a month or two, I will be able to do with my wife forever. I may be missing parties now, but when I have my own house I can blast my stereo and drink and dance until the sun comes up.

Also, I can stand over a factory pipe and inhale the smoke into my lungs, and feel like a smoker. Or better yet, I can save myself the effort of getting involved in gang violence and just jump out a window right now. You get what I'm saying?

I know a lot of teens would look at my life and say I was crazy. They'd think that any teen would live a life like mine only because he has parents who torture him. But I don't mind my parents' rules, and I've made some of the rules myself. Because when I think of my friend, I think that I could have ended up getting caught up in street life. So I'm planning to stay as far away from trouble as I can.

Curtis was 15 when he wrote this story.

Goodbye, Harlem

By Antwaun Garcia

1. I met my boy when I was 8. He was shy and something of a follower, but cool. If I cut school, he would cut with me. If I went to the candy store, he'd buy candy if he had money or he would take it.

    My boy was growing up a lot like me—on the streets all times of the night, not wanting to go home. Some days his father would hit him, or my boy and his siblings wouldn't eat, because even when their moms was sober and wanted to cook, she couldn't afford food. We became Robin Hoods, stealing from the corner store to feed the poor.

2. **Stealing to Eat**

    I wasn't thrilled about stealing to eat, but it was so easy to do it became a habit. We would walk in the store and act like family, yelling, "Mommy wanted this!" Or, "Moms needed bread for sandwiches in the morning." He would put a few items under his shirt. I would walk out first and wait for the "walk" sign. As soon as the light changed, I would open the door and he would run right through and across the street into my building.

We had tons of fun together, playing sports, chilling on the park benches eating stolen food, and laughing it all off. We were growing up in Harlem, one of the rougher neighborhoods of New York City. But even though our situation wasn't good, we found ways to enjoy life.

> **Even though I was safe, I always had this feeling that someone was going to double-cross me.**

But when I was 10, I went into foster care and moved to Queens with my aunt. It was so unexpected I didn't have a chance to say goodbye to my boy or any of my friends. Later, I wondered about him and all my family. I missed being home and wondered how they were holding up.

3. A New World

When I arrived in Queens, I felt very weird. Queens is part of New York City, but it felt like a world away. My aunt lived in a housing development with security and, between each group of four buildings, a huge circle of flowers and sprinklers. I'd never seen flowers like that in Harlem. Maybe once in a blue you would see some dude selling roses on a street corner, rolling to your window and saying, "Flowers, flowers for your loved one." But that was it. In Queens, I felt like Dorothy in *The Wizard of Oz*. I just clicked my shoes three times and I was in paradise.

Still, adapting to my new home was really difficult. My aunt had rules like, "Be home at dark." I thought, "What the f---? Home by dark?" I was used to coming home at midnight.

I also had to do chores and homework, be in bed by 9, and attend school daily, which was new for me. I hated it from the jump.

4. **Keeping Up My Game**

The biggest change was emotional. Even though I was safe, I always had this feeling that someone was going to double-cross me. I stayed cautious, my hands ready to swing. I didn't know how to react to courtesies, like someone holding doors for me or saying, "Good morning, have a nice day!" I was like, "Uh, duh... OK! Whatever!"

In Harlem, people weren't nice to me unless they knew me or my relatives. It took me a while to realize that, surprisingly, the nice people in Queens didn't have a hidden agenda.

I also found myself acting like I was back in the ghetto even though I had everything I needed. I'd steal food from stores when I had food in the house, or sell weed and bootleg CDs to make some money even though I didn't need to. I couldn't seem to get hustling out of my system. I still enjoyed the thrill and excitement of possibly getting caught, and I didn't want to lose my game. I never knew if I'd end up back in Harlem again, taking care of myself.

5. **I Could Make It**

Living with my aunt, I also felt isolated. I felt I couldn't trust anyone and had no one to really talk to. My aunt's family acted stubborn and proud, and made fun of each other for being dumb or making mistakes. I feared they thought they were too good for me. I never felt comfortable enough around them to tell them what I felt, so I kept to myself.

The older I got, the colder my heart became. For years, I isolated myself from all of my family. I barely went back to Harlem to see my extended family or my old friends. I missed my mother and father, but I was also angry at them for letting me end up in care and for being out of touch for long periods of time.

Instead, I just kept my head down and tried to take what Queens offered me. In school, I finally learned to read and write. I became a writer at a teen magazine during high school, and earned my diploma. Slowly, I began to see myself not as a kid who would need to hustle his way through life, but as someone who could make it.

6. Back on the Block

When I was in high school, I started feeling comfortable taking the train back to Harlem. One afternoon when I was 18, I saw my boy and his fam. As I approached him and his uncle on the steps of his building, they said, "Oh yo, that's Twaun. What's good, son?"

They sounded excited to see me, but the way my boy greeted me was funny. He gave me a fake pound, a quick slap, like, "Don't touch my hand." At first I didn't pay any mind to it. I was happy to see my people.

We started talking about what had been going on in the hood since I left. It was the same sad violin story: a couple of people locked up, some shot, some on crack, and a bunch either in foster care or dead. I kept my head down for a moment thinking about what they went through. It hurt.

We were quiet for a moment looking around the block. I asked my boy, "What you been up to, fam?" He said, "Nothing. Same old sh-t, different day."

> **I realized that he wasn't jealous of me because of what I was wearing, but because of the goals and dreams I believed were possible.**

I started telling him that I'd just achieved my high school diploma and planned to go to college, and that I wrote for a magazine, trying to make big moves.

Judging by his facial expression, he wasn't too thrilled to hear I was becoming successful. I noticed his posture changed and his tone got more serious. He eyed my fresh gear, my lion piece chain, the three rings on my fingers and the earrings that were shining more than 42nd Street at night. I guess he assumed I was caked up.

Then he tried to clown me in front of his brother and uncle, saying, "Oh word, so you doing your thang." He laughed like my goals in life were something humorous to him, like I was some stuck-up punk from the suburbs who wasn't hood enough to be back home.

7. **'This N-gga Changed'**

He took another pull of his cancer stick and told his uncle, "Yo, this ain't the same little kid I know. This n-gga changed."

> **Will I become the educated and professional person I hope to be, or will I just go backwards?**

Then he got in my face and said, "You p-ssy! You ain't the same cold-hearted young n-gga who used to be real and hold sh-t down."

At first I thought he was joking, but he wasn't. His eyes were squinty and his cheek muscles were tight. I was caught off guard. I never thought my boy would attack my character or throw hands with me. I thought he would be happy to see me doing my thang.

8. **My Boy Threw Hands**

I wanted to fix his lip. I was thinking, "We'll see how much I changed when I punch you in your mouth." I am a quick-tempered dude but I fell back and kept my cool. Instead of applying physical force, I played the mental game.

I replied, "So what makes me different? Because now I have a little money in my pockets? Or because you still that same cat hustling for years with no bread, struggling to make ends meet and still eating off your mom's welfare check?"

He got upset, and I could tell his family didn't like my comment either. His younger brother started to ball his fist as if to swing at me. But I continued, "Is it because you're still that same punk who needed me to fight your battles, take groceries from the store because your moms couldn't afford them?"

His uncle started cursing at me at the top of his lungs. "What! Who the f--- are you to disrespect our family!" He wouldn't stop, saying every curse word in the book.

9. Saying Goodbye

As soon as I began taking my coat off, preparing for someone to pop off, their moms came out. I felt bad for making that comment about her because she looked very ill and was coughing. She yelled, "Antwaun!" and gave me a hug and a kiss on the cheek. "Boy, I haven't seen you since you was that little angry, always fighting, peasy-headed kid, and now look at ya, you full grown and handsome."

I smirked while saying, "Thank you." She began telling me how hard it's been, especially since she'd been diagnosed with breast cancer. I could see the coldness in her brown eyes and hear the pain in her voice.

I felt for her. She was always cool with me. When her kids ate, I ate too. When I wanted to get away from my house, she always said I could come through. She was funny and smart, just not smart about getting caught in the crack game.

Then the uncle came into our convo and told her that I wasn't allowed around here no more. I gave him a cold look as my teeth scraped each other like nails scraping the blackboard. I said, "Say no more!" I gave their mother a kiss on the cheek and said it was nice to see her after so many years. She replied, "The same with you, Antwaun. I am so proud of you!"

10. Not the Same Kid Anymore

As I walked away, I felt upset that I had lost my boy who I'd been cool with for years. Thinking it over, I realized that he wasn't jealous of me because of what I was wearing, but because of the goals and dreams I believed were possible.

He had stayed behind in Harlem, and his Harlem had been what it was for me: crack, poverty, drugs, 5-0, and violence. Could I expect any more from him than to live up to his environment? Could I expect him to be happy for my good fortune when he wished to have the opportunities I was given? Don't get it twisted, I was not being cocky, but realizing I'd been fortunate.

In Queens I'd gotten the chance to start a whole new life, including going to school and living in a positive environment where I felt the freedom to become more than a punk. He was stuck living a lifestyle that he didn't choose.

11. Moving On Up?

In the last few years, I've thought a lot about that last convo with my boy. As I get older and ready to live on my own, it seems like I might end up moving back to Harlem. That feels weird, like I could wind up right back where I started, even though I've worked hard to be "movin' on up" (as they said on *The Jeffersons*).

I wonder, "When I'm on my own, will I become the educated and professional person I hope to be, or will I just go backwards?" I fear that, no matter how much success I may achieve, I could always fail at any moment.

What my boy couldn't see is that I still battle my own inner demons. I still carry around a hood mentality that makes me doubt I'll reach my dreams. Despite the hopeful picture I painted for my boy, it's hard for me to believe that long-term goals, like finishing college, will be things I'll live to achieve.

I often ask the people close to me, "Can I make it?" With reassurance from other people, I've started believing in myself, but it hasn't been easy. I'm not like many of the people I know from Queens or in college, who seem so confident of their futures.

But at least I know that hustling can never be a route to a good life. That right there should keep me on the straight path, safe from ever becoming the worst parts of the Harlem I grew up in.

Antwaun was 21 when he wrote this story.
He later became a manager at a major hardware retailer.

Following the Leader

By Anonymous

1.   Looking out the windows of the #3 subway train, I spot a familiar sign: Rockaway Ave. The doors open and I enter my world, my home: Brownsville, Brooklyn, one of the poorest neighborhoods in the country.

Slowly I walk down the stairs, then push my way through the turnstile. As I step outside, I'm greeted with the smell of weed, the sound of "Newport, come get your Newport right here," echoing through the street. Eyes gaze as I walk by. I walk fast. I'm sick of seeing those same fools drug dealing to the vulnerable or hustling on the corner.

Look straight, look ahead and surpass the negativity. Don't get sucked up in their dimension. Keep a positive mindset, don't be one of them. Don't notice a thing.

2. **My Struggling Community**

Even after so many years, my trip home still aggravates me. It's disturbing to see the black community in this state. The thieves and drug dealers hurt each other and our neighborhood to become "successful." Their pride comes in knowing that they put a loaf of bread on the table. Tell me this, though: How do you feel knowing what you had to do to get it?

African-Americans have gone through so much to gain our so-called equal rights. So why are so many of us living in run-down apartments, cooped up in projects, depending on welfare, stashed up in prison, and stuck in segregated communities like Brownsville?

> **Very few drug dealers make more than minimum wage.**

To find out, I talked with a sociologist at Columbia University, Sudhir Venkatesh, who spent years observing Chicago drug dealers' daily struggles to get rich or die trying. A gang member on his way to prison even gave Venkatesh detailed notes he kept about his hustling business, including how much the gang paid everyone from lookouts to leaders.

3. **Dealing Pays Badly**

People deal drugs because they believe there's tremendous opportunity to go from rags to riches, Venkatesh said. But in fact, only very few drug dealers make more than minimum wage. The gang leader Venkatesh met paid himself about $100,000 a year— or $66 an hour. (Sounds like a lot, but that's about what some experienced, unionized teachers and nurses make, when you include benefits like health care. And bankers and lawyers can make much more.) Even worse, the gang leader paid the three guys beneath him about $7 an hour and the street level dealers an average of $3.30 an hour—less than minimum wage, which was about $4.25 at that time.

"If you look at 100 drug dealers, 99 will make less than minimum wage. One will make a lot of money. That's the reality on the streets," Venkatesh told me. "It's an illusion that people have that they're going to make a lot of money. That's only the leader driving a fancy car."

Venkatesh said that he believes teens don't choose a life of crime so much as find it difficult to get a decent job. Many African-Americans and Latinos grow up in poor neighborhoods like Brownsville where the schools usually do a bad job of preparing kids for decent jobs or college, he said. Most high-paying factory and union jobs have disappeared, so it's much harder to support a family without an education these days. And college has gotten very expensive.

4. No Way Out?

Racial discrimination and segregation also make it harder for minorities to start legitimate businesses, because many banks are unlikely to give loans to people who want to start businesses in poor neighborhoods, Venkatesh said.

Diane Hawkins-Bonaventure, deputy executive director of the nonprofit East New York Development Corporation, helps people who were on welfare get jobs. "It's always difficult for people to find jobs, but I work in the minority community, with people who've been on public assistance. Many of them are lacking minimal education, like a GED, and have low or no marketable job skills, so it's really hard," she said.

Many of the drug dealers Venkatesh met seemed miserable standing out on the corner but couldn't see a way out. "Drug dealers are very, very scared. They don't like standing on a corner, they don't like carrying a gun. They don't know what's happening in their lives, but they're too scared to tell anybody. It's hard for them to ask for help," he said.

Poor teens get stuck on corners or in jail because we see the successful drug dealers flossing their platinum chains and spinning chromes on their Cadillacs, and we follow them. In other neighborhoods, kids see people become rich by going to business school and putting on a suit.

5. **Education Pays**

One day I walked through Brooklyn Heights, a wealthy, mostly white neighborhood that's also in New York City. I wondered what kind of dreams the kids I know might have if they got off the train there. The neighborhood was almost picture perfect—the sidewalks weren't smothered with litter, the houses were old but not worn down, there wasn't any graffiti on the buildings.

I felt like I could breathe. I didn't have to worry about getting into an argument with any chickenheads. The streets weren't crowded, and when I spotted people they were minding their own damn business. I had no worries about my safety at all.

In a neighborhood like that, it's easy for kids to see the connection between getting an education and making money. In Brooklyn Heights, 58% of people over age 25 had at least a college degree, and the average household income was $56,300, according to the 2000 Census. Compare that to Brownsville, where only 8% had a college degree and the average household income was about $21,000. There aren't a lot of role models in my neighborhood to show kids like me the path to success.

6. **Following What We See**

The reality is that most children follow the examples of their parents and the people around them. That came home to me when I visited Norwalk, a small city in Connecticut. Riding the commuter train, I was shocked to look out the window and see enormous houses and green lawns. I usually see places like that on television, but here I was just an hour away from Manhattan. It all looked so beautiful.

When I talked to several groups of suburban teens, it struck me that all of them were expecting to go to college. For them, college wasn't an option—it was a must. They were probably so confident about college because their parents went, or their friends' parents went, and everyone around them expected them to go.

A lot of the kids in my school view college as a luxury. Everyone around us is doing so poorly that we tell ourselves, "I guess I can't break through these barriers," and we don't dare to try.

7. Another Path, Through Activism

When I asked Venkatesh and Hawkins-Bonaventure how they thought poor neighborhoods could change, they agreed that poor people of all ages need to come together and demand more from our government and business leaders, like a higher minimum wage and more job training.

"Advocate for change—change in schools, change in police patrols. Become more involved in what's going on in the community," Hawkins-Bonaventure said. "Go to your state representatives, city rep-resentatives, federal represen-tatives, and let them know what's needed."

> **The reality is that most children follow the examples of their parents and the people around them.**

They also agreed that poor teens can succeed if they get help from after-school programs, social workers, and mentors who can show them a different path. Organizations like the East New York Development Corporation offer programs that encourage youth to stay out of trouble and in school. Their large after-school program offers help with homework and SATs, GED preparation for young adults, and a safe environment for youth after school.

8. Beyond the Barriers

Although I grew up in a hostile neighborhood, I've sought out other opportunities, like the debate team at my school and an after-school writing program. These experiences have shown me that I can look beyond the barriers I see between my dreams and me.

I know life can be really hard, and the future can seem like it's got nothing in it. It hasn't been easy trying to keep my head on in school so I can make it out. But I've used my disgust with my neighborhood and our society to become the total opposite. I wish that it could be easier for others to do the same.

The author later graduated from high school and went to college, while working several part-time jobs.

Chapter 3

How Do We
Define Ourselves?

Crewsin' for a Bruisin'

By Troy Shawn Welcome

1. **A**re you in a crew? If you are, you know that a lot of crews live a fast life and their actions can lead to prison or worse.

For starters, the more people you're with, the more attention you're going to attract. And then most teenagers aren't conscious of what they're doing half the time and don't take the time to reflect or anticipate. Reflecting on what I've done or imagining all the possibilities of a situation before it happens is how I notice my mistakes or avoid them before they can negatively affect my life and my future.

Thinking about my own experiences in a crew led me to make up this story of how a typical crew might get themselves into trouble.

*   *   *   *   *

It's Friday night and the crew is chillin' on the corner. Jay, who's known for stealing cars, doing stick-ups, and shoplifting when he's hungry, is sitting on a car rolling a blunt.

Rob, nicknamed Nitti for the character from the movie *The Untouchables*, is passing around a forty to be tapped.

Jeff, who's the one that everybody goes to when they want to discuss an idea for a jack, is coming down the block. They call him the Intelligent Hoodlum, the brain of the crew.

Danny, Chris, and Paul, who are always there for the blunt but for the beef they always front, are scattered on the corner. You only see Danny, Chris, and Paul when the rest of the crew needs them for something.

"Yo, Jay!" says Rob.

"What yo? I'm trying to roll this!" answers Jay.

"Yo, here comes Jeff," says Rob.

As Jeff approaches the corner, a group of guys who are new to the area are walking towards him. Jeff walks through the crowd and gets shoved around like a bumper car. He turns around and confronts the last guy to bump him.

2. The Initial Spark

"What's the problem?" he asks.

"N-gga, you got something to say!" someone says from the middle of the crowd. "If you want it, it's here."

These guys have no idea that Jeff's boys are right on the corner. And Jeff's crew hasn't seen what's happening down the block.

"Yo Rob, I thought you said that Jeff was coming. Where he at?" says Jay as he seals the blunt.

"He's right...(Rob looks down the block.) Yo, yo some fools is tryin' to mess with my man," he says as he grabs a gun from his car and runs towards Jeff.

"Right where n-gga? Oh sh-t!" Jay throws the blunt into the car, grabs his weapon. "Yo D'...yo Paul...yo Chris...it's on...it's on!" He shouts and runs over to Jeff.

Danny, Chris, and Paul can see what's going on but they don't immediately follow Jay and Rob.

3. **The Louder the Mouth. . .**

"Yo, it's mad n-ggas over there," says Danny. "Yo, c'mon Chris, you going or what?"

"Yo, I think this n-gga Chris is a little p-ssyfied!" says Paul laughing. "Yo, c'mon ya'll, I don't know about you but I ain't going out like a herb."

That's what he says, but what he's actually thinking is: "These n-ggas could beat my ass. I don't think I could handle these guys. But if I don't go then everybody will think that I'm a herb. But I'm not. Forget it, I'll go, but if anything happens I'm out."

> **It's usually the guys that boast the most who are hiding something.**

It's usually the guys that boast the most who are hiding something, because they're not secure with themselves. So while they're saying, "Don't mess with me cause I'll bus' ya ass!" they're thinking, "If this kid hits me, I don't know what I'm going to do."

Jay, Rob and Jeff are about to get into a fight with the opposing crew. Chris, Paul and Danny are waiting in the background.

*   *   *   *   *

4. **Stop and Think**

Now stop and think for a minute about what just happened. Both crews feel that they are being disrespected. Jeff was bumped around and no one said as much as a "pardon me." The person who did the bumping feels like he's being challenged. And he must prove to his boys and to Jeff that he's no herb—that no one is allowed to test him. Meanwhile Jeff's crew sees one of their own outnumbered. How could this whole thing have been avoided?

One way is if Jeff had realized that walking through the middle of the opposing crew could cause problems. Some people will think this is the herb's way out—but would you rather take the herb's way out or the body-bag out?

He also could have talked his way through it. I'm not suggesting that he should say, "Chill yo, you the man, I don't wanna mess with you," or, "Alright, you got it and I don't want it." There are other ways to talk through a situation.

> **How many more of us must die, be caged, or be crippled for saying, "What you looking at?"**

He could just say, "Excuse you, my man," and keep walking. Someone might say something to him, but he doesn't have to get into a confrontation. He could just keep walking and pretend that nothing happened.

I know some of you are still saying that you don't want to go out like a sucka. But if you're secure with yourself, you won't need to prove that you deserve respect from a stranger in the street.

5. **A Prelude to Death**

And then there's the problem of the guns. If these people didn't have weapons they would handle it differently. Weapons, and guns especially, are a fool's way of dealing with his problems. They give people the nerve to go out and kill—and to get themselves and their friends killed. Remember that it's better to live to talk about what happened, than to die and be remembered as the guy who got slaughtered for a ridiculous cause—a bump in the night.

I want my peers—especially my African-American brothers—to start thinking more about their actions and the consequences of those actions. Why was your boy hurt the other day?

Did he lose his life or end up in a wheelchair for a stare, bump, or battle of the egos? How many more of us must die, be caged, or be crippled for saying, "What you looking at?"

When guns, buddah, and forties become a way of life—it's a prelude to death!

Here are a few of your typical characters in a crew:

6. **The Gangsta:** He walks down the streets, strutting his stuff as if he controls everything and everyone in sight—the one who's always saying, "Whatever, I don't give a f---!" He gives the crew all its ideas. He might say, "Yo, let's do this n-gga" or "What's those n-ggas looking at?" or, "I feel like jacking somebody, yo."

    The rest of the crew almost always goes along with whatever this character wants to do, because if they challenge his corrupt ideas they might be called a p-ssy. He lives life for money, women, violence, and more money. If someone tries to diss him, he must get respect from them before he walks on. (He never got respect or real love as a child; to fill that void he tries to demand it from others.) He's very street smart, but things don't always run smoothly for this character.

    He has to fight to maintain his position. And because he's acting mostly on his emotions, he lacks the ability to *reflect*.

7. **The Intelligent Hoodlum:** Every crew has at least one of these. He uses his intelligence to improve the schemes of the crew. Any time that the crew decides to do something, everybody instinctively waits for him to give his opinion. He's usually the one who looks at both sides of a situation, sees what can go wrong, and how to improve the plan.

    If the crew has beef, he's the one who thinks more about how to get out of the situation so they can come back to get revenge, rather than how to prove who's the bigger man. After he has improved their present scheme, he almost always goes along with the plan.

8. **Joe Borderline:** He lives the crew life but doesn't want to die from it. He's better at anticipating the consquences, and this makes him cautious. He loves action but sees the consequences that action brings. He enjoys alcohol but sees that every time they drink the crew gets into trouble. He wants to have a better life, but doesn't really want to leave the fellas.

    If there is beef, he's in the background so he doesn't start anything. If he has to fight he will, but only after the rest of the crew decides to. He keeps quiet because he doesn't want to do anything that might start any trouble and he doesn't want to seem like a herb and say something like, "Yo, let's drop it!" And he's not a herb—he's just confused.

9. **The Herb:** He's a follower. A herb, by my definition, is someone who compromises his or her morals for the satisfaction of his friends. He does what the majority of the crew wants to do. He's the one that ends up being used, because he has no backbone.

    In the case of any beef, these characters are either the loud ones or overly quiet. If someone says, "Yo, f--- these n-ggas," they'd say, "Yo man, I'm saying f--- these n-ggas. Yo, we gonna do something or not?" If they weren't herbs, they wouldn't wait for anyone else to start something, they'd start it themselves. They always wait for somebody to speak first, to make sure that they have back up.

    This kind of herb makes a lot of noise when he is with his boys, but doesn't usually do it when he's alone. The beast only comes out when he's with the crew.

    That sums it up. Each of these guys thinks he's an individual—free to come and go as he pleases. In fact, each is a prisoner of his role.

Troy was 19 when he wrote this story, and had recently left the street life behind. After graduating from college he became a teacher at his old high school, and is now a principal.

Glossary

Beef: an argument or reason to fight

Blunt: a cigar that's been hollowed out and filled with marijuana

Buddah: marijuana

Front: act falsely tough

Forty: a 40-ounce bottle of malt liquor

Herb: a nerd

Jack: to steal

Mad: a lot

Color Me Different

By Jamal Greene

1.   I am black. Yet, since I was 12, I've gone to a school almost totally devoid of black people. I don't speak in slang. I don't listen to rap or reggae and, try as I might, I have at best a 50-50 chance of converting a lay-up. Except for the fact that I'm not white, I am not all that different from a stereotypical white kid from the suburbs.

Because of this, when I'm around other black people I usually feel a certain distance between us. And so do they. For example, this past summer I took a journalism workshop at New York University. After it was over, I was on the phone with one of the girls in the workshop, a black girl, and we got to talking about first impressions. She said that for about the first week of the workshop, she was saying to herself, "What's wrong with this guy? Is he white or something?" She said that I talked like a "cracker" (as she put it) and she made a lot of offhand remarks about me not being a "real" black person. It irritated me that this girl thought that just because I didn't speak "black English," I was not a genuine black person.

2. **I Don't Talk the Talk**

I have often heard people criticize Paul Olden, a New York Yankees announcer, for the way he speaks. He's black, but you would never know it from the way he talks. They say he's trying to be white. I don't "sound black" either and I'm not trying to be anything but who I am. It's just the way I talk. Black people who speak standard English don't do it because they want to dissociate themselves from other black people but because they grew up hearing English spoken that way.

Just look at the English boxer Lennox Lewis. He's black but his accent is as British as can be. Is he "trying to be English" and denying his black roots? Of course not. He just grew up around people who had British accents.

3. **No Rhythm**

I don't dance like a lot of other black people either. I never learned to move my hips and legs the way most kids you see at parties are able to. I lose the beat if I have to move more than two body parts at once and so my dancing tends to get a little repetitive.

When I go to parties with black people I often find myself sitting at the table drinking a Coke while everybody else is dancing. "Why aren't you dancing?!" people ask. And then when I do get on the dance floor, the same people sneer at me. "What's wrong with you?" they say. "Why do you just keep doing the same thing over and over again?"

Contrary to popular belief, black people aren't born with the ability to dance and play basketball. Even though I have speed and leaping ability, I can't drive to the hole without losing my dribble. Those skills have to be learned and perfected with practice. It only seems like they are innate because the black community in America is culturally very close-knit and people share the same interests.

4. **Out of Their League**

Another thing that constitutes "blackness" in a lot of people's minds is an interest in or a feeling of pride and identification with things historically black. I collected baseball cards until I was 15. I had a pretty substantial collection for a kid. At least, I thought I did. One afternoon, my cousins came over to my house and were looking at my baseball cards.

"Do you have any Jackie Robinson cards?" one of them asked.

"Of course not," I answered.

They were visibly displeased with that response. Of course in my mind I knew that the reason I didn't have any Jackie Robinson cards was the same reason why I didn't have any Ted Williams or Mickey Mantle or Joe DiMaggio cards. I just didn't have the money for Jackie Robinson. Even if I were going to spend that money on baseball cards, I would buy a Mickey Mantle card before I would buy a Jackie Robinson card of the same price. Jackie may have been the first black major leaguer but Mickey hit home runs and home runs increase in value faster than historical novelty. It's that simple. But my cousins thought that the reason I didn't have any Jackie Robinson cards was because I didn't like black players as much as white players.

> **She made a lot of offhand remarks about me not being a "real" black person.**

5. **An Added Responsibility**

My family has always had a problem with me liking baseball—a game that did not integrate until 1947—as much as I do. They keep getting me these Negro League postcards because they are worried that I don't know enough about the subject. And they're right. But then again, sports enthusiasts in general don't know enough about the Negro Leagues. My family feels very strongly that as a black sports fan, I should feel an added responsibility to know about black baseball players. If I don't learn about them, they say, then nobody will.

Minorities are often called upon to be the spokespeople for their races. The only black kid in the class is almost always asked to speak when the subjects of slavery or the civil rights movement come up. The question is, does he have a responsibility to know more about issues pertaining to blacks than his white classmates? I would like to think that he doesn't.

> **By one definition I'm not black at all. But I was black the last time I looked in the mirror.**

If we really believe that everyone should be treated equally, then ideally my Jewish friends should be expected to know just as much about black history as I do. Of course I should know more about the Negro Leagues than I do now, but so should a white baseball fan or a Japanese baseball fan or a polka-dot baseball fan.

6. **I'm a Square Peg...**

So I guess I don't fit in with the black people who speak in slang, dance with a lot of hip motion, and hang out with an all-black crowd. And I don't feel any added responsibility to learn about black history or go out and associate with more black people either. Nor do I fit in with blacks who try as hard as they can to separate themselves from blacks altogether, vote Republican, and marry white women. I wouldn't do that either.

Even though I grew up playing wiffle ball with white kids in Park Slope instead of basketball with black kids in Bed Stuy, even though I go to a school with very few blacks, and even though most of my friends are white and Asian, I can't say that I feel completely at home with white people either. Achieving racial equality is a process that still has a long way to go. Blacks were slaves for hundreds of years. And we were legally inferior to whites up until just a couple generations ago. Blacks may have achieved equality before the law, but it will take another few generations to achieve full social equality.

7. **The Invisible Line**

There is still a stigma attached to interracial relationships, for example, both romantic and otherwise. Whenever I'm around the parents of white friends, I get the sense that they see me not as "that nice kid who is friends with my son or daughter" but rather as "that nice black kid who is friends with my son or daughter." There is still a line that certain people are unwilling to cross.

So after all this analysis, I'm still confused about what it means to be black. What is race, anyway? According to Webster's dictionary, race is "a class or kind of people unified by a community of interests, habits, or characteristics." Well, anyone who's ever called me or any other black person "white on the inside" because we didn't fit their stereotype can look at that definition and claim victory. "There it is, right in the dictionary," they're saying. "Black is an attitude, not just a color."

By that definition I'm not black at all. But I was black the last time I looked in the mirror. So I went back to the dictionary and found that Webster's has another definition for race: "a division of mankind possessing traits that are transmissible by descent and sufficient to characterize it as a distinct human type."

8. **Who to Believe?**

Wait a minute! Does that mean that a black person is anyone with dark skin, full lips, a broad nose, and coarse hair? These are traits transmissible by descent and distinct to black people. By the second definition, to be black means to have these physical characteristics. Speaking in slang and dancing well are not genetic—they are cultural.

Which definition is right? I would like to think that it is the second. I would like to think that race is nothing more than the color of your skin, but clearly in most people's minds it's more than that. I feel distanced from blacks because I am black but don't act the part and I feel distanced from whites because I act white but don't look the part. As long as other people expect me to act a certain way because of the way I look, or to look a certain way because of the way I act, I will continue to be something of an outcast because I defy their prejudices.

Society has different expectations of blacks and whites, and becomes uncomfortable if any of us strays from those expectations. Just ask anybody who's ever picked me for two-on-two just because I was black.

Jamal wrote this story when he was 16. He later graduated from Harvard. He then became a sports journalist, went to law school, and clerked for Justice John Paul Stevens on the U.S. Supreme Court. He is now a law school professor.

Getting Ghetto

By Fred Wagenhauser

1.   **W**ould you be interested to hear another Eminem story about a white kid who's been through so much? White kids trying to be ghetto—it sounds like an "Animorph" book, but it's a reality. I'm white, I live in the projects, I can rap, and all my life I've made friends with danger and deceit.

My roots in "urban culture" started while I was just a kid living in New Jersey with my Aunt Trish and Uncle Lenny. That side of the family was mixed, and threw me into a world of hip-hop and r&b.

I liked rap from the jump. I could vibe the lyrics about how hard it was living in the streets because my family had to scrounge to make ends meet. As for r&b, I loved the way the artists sang about love and loss.

2. From Peace to Chaos

Now, my family has never been stereotypically white. By that I mean acting like you got a bad smell under your nose, have never been arrested, have a lot of money, and stay away from the projects. My family is not like that. We don't have money, we're not snobs, and some of us have been in foster care or locked up.

My brother bangs with the six (rolls with a crew) and he's always in trouble. My mother was in foster care when she was little, and when people meet her they know she's real. One time we were riding in the car when a Snoop Dogg throwback came on. My mom got excited and started to sing along with Snoop and Dre. She's gangsta.

> **I felt that because I was white I had to be the toughest and meanest kid on the wing to get respect.**

When I was 9 we moved from Jersey to New York, where my mom grew up. When I got to the block, all I heard playing was reggae, Spanish music, and of course blazin' hip-hop and r&b. Jersey had been peaceful and quiet, but New York was noisy and crowded and chaotic. I loved it.

3. A Nerd Turns "Wigger"

When September came, 3rd grade was cool and fun but there was one problem: I was a nerd, from how I talked to how I dressed. My family never really had money like that, so I was in Payless kicks and some Wal-Mart clothes. I was always made fun of.

The next year my mom said I was going to a new school. I was happy. Maybe it would be a new start for me. But again, the same things: I had no gear and I was a nerd. What friends I did make wanted me to change.

"Fred, why do you wear such tight pants?" Harry asked one day.

"My mother doesn't have it like that," I told him. I felt embarrassed and annoyed, because it's nobody's business why I dress the way I do. But eventually it started to eat at me on the inside.

I asked my mother if I could get new jeans so I wouldn't get picked on. The next time my family took me shopping, I picked out the baggy jeans instead of the "nut huggers." I was so happy because I got more respect.

Then the tables turned. One day at lunch when I was 11 years old, my friends (who were all black and Latino, like most of the kids in my school) told me I was a "wigger." I didn't know what that word meant until Harry told me it was a white person trying to be black.

That's when I realized that some of the things I did to fit in are not stereotypically black, but stereotypically ghetto.

4. Proving Myself

Then, when I was 13 years old, I beat up a kid in my middle school. I was dealing with a lot of problems and got sent to a residential treatment center, St. Mary's. In that environment, everyone assumed that since I was white and smart I was a nerd. But when they heard my poetry about my life struggles, it wiped the smirk off their faces.

> **Learning to fight, deal, and battle rap—those are not the only things I want to learn in life.**

Then I got sent to a lockdown in upstate New York. I don't like to fight but I will if I have to. So I was fighting a lot just to prove to everyone I wasn't an ass. I felt that because I was white I had to be the toughest and meanest kid on the wing to get respect. I had to learn how to freestyle and battle rap and keep up on the new slang coming in. All this just so I could watch TV in peace.

One time, the whole wing was bored so a few kids started to battle rap. James said, "Come on, Fred, it's just like poetry."

I tried and messed up but it was cool so I practiced. I started to speak what was on my mind in front of people.

5. **Finding My Voice**

Those experiences taught me to use my voice. I've always been a really shy person. I'm not good in crowds. In general, I really don't believe in myself. When I found out I could survive in lockdown and that I had a little flow, my confidence rose.

But now that I'm right on the borderline of adulthood, I feel I need to change certain aspects of my ghetto ways. I have to calm down a lot. I get into fights on the regular and

> **I want to show people color doesn't define me.**

in the past six months I've been to the bookings three times. Plus, I don't have a real job, I'm not in school, and I'm on the verge of homelessness. It's real hard.

Sometimes I feel in my bones that if I don't get out of my neighborhood soon, someone's going to get hurt. I don't want to do that. I want to expand my mind. Learning about hip-hop style and music, and to fight, deal, and battle rap—those are not the only things I want to learn in life.

6. **The Best of Both Worlds**

I'm hoping to take my ass to college far away from the Lowa Deck (the Lower East Side, a rough neighborhood in New York City). But I wonder if I can go to school far from here, and if I do, am I really going to calm down on the criminal stuff? I'm not gonna sit here, lie and say "I'm gonna change" when I don't know if I will.

I want the best of both worlds. I want to be able to do my thing on job interviews and amaze college professors with my vast intellect, and on the flip side, walk through the projects because I know mad people from different walks of life.

I want to show people color doesn't define me. I want to bring my hunger and the ability to adapt that I got from the streets and apply it to making a straight life. That's my uniqueness. But dealing and getting locked up? Nah. I have to be able to control my anger and get out of the damn ghetto.

I fear losing my voice and my confidence. I also fear I might get in too deep and bang, I'm caught up again. But I hope that understanding the dangers of living crooked will help me find a new way to stand up and be me.

Fred was 21 when he wrote this story. He later moved to a different neighborhood and got a job delivering newspapers.

I'm Not What You Expect Me to Be

By Jordan Yue

1. "**Y**ou're good at math, right?"

Both Asian and non-Asian classmates have said that to me, throwing it out in casual conversation as we're walking to class.

Actually, I'm just OK at math. But it bothers me that they seem to think I'd be a math whiz just because I'm Chinese-American and there's a common idea that Chinese people—and Asians in general—are good at math. I feel like people have certain assumptions about me simply because when they look at me, they see "Chinese" or "Asian."

The stereotype goes beyond math skills. Asians are called the "model minority" because we're the minority group that people say succeeds best in America; according to the stereotype, we work hard, stay quiet, and don't cause trouble. An Asian student is valedictorian? No big surprise. According to the stereotype, we're both disciplined and naturally smart.

2. **Respect for Scholars**

It's not like the stereotype comes from nowhere. In Chinese culture, for example, education and discipline are very important. Throughout Chinese history, scholars were the most respected people in society. Martial arts, tai chi, and Confucian principles also teach discipline, so it makes sense that discipline plays an important part in the culture.

That might sound good to you, but the flip side is that we're also considered sexless (or at least the guys are), socially inept, and easy to pick on. And even the "good" parts of the stereotype bug me, because I feel like people look at me and automatically see someone I'm not.

3. **Pressure at Home, Too**

Now, I'm not gonna front. In some ways I do fit this stereotype, at least the academic part. I go to Bronx Science, a top-rated high school in New York City that you have to take a test to get into. More than 40% of my school is Asian.

But in other ways, I feel like the stereotype isn't me, and even if I wanted to be that way and tried, I couldn't do it. I'm also mad at the reality behind the stereotype; at home, I get the kind of pressure to do well that really is common in Asian families. I feel like both outsiders and my own parents expect me to be the "model minority."

4. **More American Than Chinese**

Ever since I can remember, I haven't matched people's expectations. I'm a third generation Asian-American—this means it was my great-grandparents who immigrated here—and in lots of ways I feel more American than Chinese. I don't speak Chinese. I like basketball. I listen mostly to hip-hop, reggae, blues, rock, and r&b. I hate going to school. I curse like a sailor. I'm interested in the latest sneakers coming out. I'm your typical American teen.

Back when I was a young'un, I wasn't treated warmly by most of the Asian kids. You see, my area of Flushing, Queens, is mostly first and second generation Koreans and some Chinese. Most of the kids' parents were immigrants, and some of the kids were, too.

I didn't understand Chinese and I didn't speak with an accent, so they often accused me of trying to be white. Whether it was at school or in the neighborhood playing ball, they made it clear that I didn't fit in. I did have friends, who varied in race, but I was a lunchroom table-hopper, trying out different groups to see if I fit in.

5. Rebel Heroes

At home, my parents expected me to be a good student. An 80 on a test wasn't good enough. It sometimes seemed that they wanted me to exceed some unstated expectation. For the most part this didn't bother me. I did my work in school and didn't cause too many problems. Up through 7th grade I was relatively obedient and performed well throughout the year.

Still, my heroes were loner rebel characters like Han Solo, a leader of the Rebel Alliance in *Star Wars*, and Wolverine of the *X-Men*. Wolverine is hotheaded, and always seems pissed off because he was either misunderstood or mistreated. I looked up to these rebels, who were much more fascinating than the do-gooder, wholesome characters like Superman.

> **Even the "good" parts of the stereotype bug me, because I feel like people look at me and see someone I'm not.**

In 8th grade, I started acting up in class. I didn't know what exactly was bothering me; I just felt 8th grade was a waste of time. I was disruptive and made inappropriate comments. I felt that I was funny, even if classmates were telling me to shut up. My teachers started sending notes home to my parents. My parents got mad and yelled at me, so then I'd yell back.

6. ## Mad at Parents, Mad at Self

Part of me was having fun, but another part of me was angry. I didn't want to be obedient and quiet. I was angry at my parents, who I felt were blaming me without acknowledging their own contributions to my behavior. But I was angry at myself, too, because I had done well the year before and I just couldn't see why I was doing poorly this year.

I felt that nobody understood me and worse, no one cared to try; they all had their pre-formed ideas about who I was supposed to be.

> **I didn't have to choose between the total rebel or the total goody two-shoes. I could be a balance of both.**

The worse I felt, the angrier I got, and the more trouble I got in. I was acting out and not handing in my work, and my parents were furious over the letters they were getting about my cutting class. I wasn't happy with myself, but my parents yelling at me so much didn't exactly motivate me to make the right choices.

I felt that I didn't fit in at home or at school, but I didn't know why or how to change the situation. Then, the summer after 8th grade, I picked up a book called *Eastern Standard Time*, which is about Asian culture in America.

The book brought to my attention the "model minority" stereotype and opened up a world of thought for me. The book said that the image of a studious, disciplined achiever was something that grew out of Asian values and suggested that it's both positive and negative.

7. ## Rethinking Expectations

At first I thought I liked the idea of the model minority stereotype, since it meant that society expected me to succeed; I wasn't feeling like anyone expected me to succeed after my miserable time in 8th grade.

Yet when I gave it more thought, I realized how bad the stereotype was. It put down other minorities by implying that none work as hard as Asians. And it labeled me as something I wasn't: a focused overachiever who doesn't rock the boat.

Learning about the model minority stereotype made me realize why so many Asians I knew were stressed about grades. The book helped me think about the expectations I was resisting at school and at home; it was like people expected me to get good grades and be obedient just because I was Asian—not because I was Jordan. It made me angry at the stereotype, and a little less angry at myself.

8. **Nearly Suspended**

Still, I entered high school with the same rebellious attitude I'd had through junior high. I was loud and obnoxious in my classes and was almost suspended for throwing a book at my global history teacher (though really I was passing it to its owner across the room—through the air).

That spring I was diagnosed with a mild case of attention deficit disorder (ADD), which means I'm easily distracted and have a hard time concentrating.

Finding out about my ADD made me feel like I stood out even more. How stereotypically Asian could I be when I had to take medication just to sit quietly in class and learn? But the medication helped me focus, and I didn't feel the same impulse to blurt out wise-ass comments in class. I felt more in control, and in a way, that made me less angry.

9. **Friends I Can Chill With**

Since I wasn't as obnoxious in class, things got cooler with my classmates. Even though I wasn't the model minority child my parents wanted me to be—and I was still mad at them for expecting me to be that way—I wasn't feeling so badly about myself.

And in high school, I found the group of people I'm most cool with and comfortable around, who happen mostly to be black and Hispanic. Two of my best friends—Ian and Ptah, who are black—were more focused than I was about school, which was a good influence on me when I was angry over yet another failed test.

I related to them because they know how to balance doing well in school with being able to get down, chill, and party on the side. I didn't have to choose between the total rebel or the total goody two-shoes. I could be a balance of both.

Ptah told me once that he thinks the stereotypes Asians have to deal with aren't bad. He feels the stereotypes blacks are subjected to, like being thugs and drug dealers, are much worse.

10. Stereotypes Get in the Way

I understand his point of view. But I still don't like being boxed in by a list of assumptions that don't fit me, which is what the model minority stereotype of Asians does.

The problem with any stereotype is that it gets in the way of people seeing you as an individual. Stereotypes are like an outside skin that people should learn to see past.

> **The stereotype put down other minorities by implying that none work as hard as Asians.**

People are deep and complex. Everyone has a story to tell, something different to say. Everyone wants recognition, and labeling people with stereotypes makes the individual disappear.

11. Calmer at Home

After freshman year, my parents lowered their standards for me. They accept that I'm going down my own path—which does include college, even if it's not the Ivy League as my mom was hoping. Things are calmer at home, which is a relief.

In some ways, I feel like I've escaped the stereotype. I'm happier being myself, kicking it with people who accept me for whoever I am.

It's funny how easy it is to stereotype each other when most of us want to be seen as the individuals we are. I'm Jordan: the loud, obnoxious, college-bound Asian-American kid from Flushing, Queens, who has something to say.

Jordan wrote this story when he was 17.
He went on to college, majoring in public relations.

The Soundtrack of My Life

By Otis Hampton

1.   **T**eachers, subjects, classrooms, schoolbooks, friends: They're always there as you move through school, but they're always changing. For me, music is like that—a constant presence that changes as I change. At first, music connected me to other people, but then it separated me from others and even, for a time, from myself.

    In the 3rd grade, most of us liked the same type of music: pop. Pop music gives listeners a chance to release the real singer inside of them, and that's what it did for my friends Darrel, Stephen, Samuel, Glenn, and me.

    The five of us especially enjoyed The Backstreet Boys, 'NSYNC, and 98 Degrees, boy bands that were wildly popular at the time. We thought it was funny that they sang like a bunch of girls, and we also liked the beats and the clever dance moves. We started our own cover band and called ourselves "Black Kids," since all of us were African-American.

We started singing the songs that everyone knew and dancing the way the boys in the videos did. We pretended to have solo records, arguments, and resignations from the group. Other kids at school played along by pretending to be interviewers, talk-show hosts, and even kindergarten "paparazzi." We would hold group meetings to discuss boy band problems.

Stephen would demand, "How come you and Darrel get all the solos while we're the back-up dancers?" Glenn stomped out once after shouting, "You'll be hearing from my lawyer … as soon as I find out where I can get one."

Eventually the five of us quit the group and went back to just being fans. It was the last time being a music fan was simple for me, and it would be a long time before I'd be popular at school again.

2. On to Harder Stuff

One day I was sitting at home and felt the floor in my room start to vibrate. I knew for a fact that nobody in the house had a foot that big. My adoptive mom called to me from her room, "Tell Brian to turn that music down. I'm on the phone." I made my way downstairs cautiously.

Brian is my mom's biological child, and much older than me—in his 30s. I've known Brian since I was 5, when I came to their home from foster care. They adopted me a few years later, and around that time Brian's (our) father died. I was 7. I had loved my new father very much, and I reacted to his death by getting into a lot of fights and other trouble.

Since then, Brian had taken on a stern father role with me. If I got into trouble at school, there was no explaining my side of the story. All I would get out of Brian was, "I don't care who started it—if the teacher says 'sit down,' you sit down," or "I don't want to hear it," or my personal favorite, "You are such a liar."

It was hard standing up to Brian. Nevertheless, I had to do what my mom told me. I yelled out: "Brian! Mom said to turn the stereo down!" Usually, I would flee as quickly as possible from him, but this time I pressed my ear to his door.

The guitars, bass, and drums made me think of an action movie starring Vin Diesel. A voice that sounded like it came from an insane asylum screamed out: "Everything you say to me/ Takes me one step closer to the edge—and I'm about to break!" This was hardcore aggression and anger—this was Linkin Park.

It spoke to me more than the heartbreak in pop music. It sounded like the singer was going through a rough time. I guess I related that to the tough time I had trying to communicate with my family—among other things that made me angry.

3. **Messages in the Music**

Pretty soon, I was watching music videos with my brother, from bands like Mudvayne, Tool, and Stone Temple Pilots. We both liked screaming along with the songs and nodding our heads rhythmically. We'd also discuss what we liked or disliked about each track, and soon we started talking about other things, too. Brian even commended me on my achievements in school. I was very happy with our new relationship, and hard rock music seemed to have started it.

I started asking my mom for CDs from Linkin Park and other bands like P.O.D. (Payable On Death) and Disturbed. Lyrics like P.O.D.'s "I feel so alive for the very first time" or Linkin Park's "If I could change, I would / Take back the pain, I would / Retrace every wrong move that I made, I would" fit with what I was feeling at that age. Listening to these songs made me feel I wasn't the only one who was distressed.

In a way, I had grown up at a young age. Right after my dad died, I let out my anger in fighting, but since then I'd taken control of myself. What I was angry at now was the disobedience I saw everywhere I turned: little kids disrespecting their parents and defacing their schools; teenagers stealing junk food and sneakers; and everyone cursing in every sentence. I felt isolated from those kids.

Brian told me time and time again about the consequences of disrespect for others and myself. Having spent several years in foster care, I knew better than most kids that you could end up alone and unprotected. The song "World So Cold" by Mudvayne confirmed what I already knew about how harsh this world can be as a result of things like neglect and ignorance.

4. **Changing Faces**

As I moved on to middle school, I became the target of students who characterized themselves as "gang members." They picked on me because I seemed different. Maybe it was because my pants weren't sagged down below my underwear, or maybe because I speak without slurring my speech. Whatever the reason was, these wannabe thugs put me through my own personal hell.

This "gang" regularly beat me up and stuffed me into lockers. As the school year wore on, I tried not to care. I ignored them as much as I could. Some people say that rock music only talks about loneliness and sadness, but that worked for me. Music helped me survive this time because I figured out a way to cancel out all the crap I'd been taking: put on my headphones and keep on walking.

> **I figured out a way to cancel out all the crap I'd been taking: Put on my headphones and keep on walking.**

All my old friends, including my former bandmates, had become young thugs themselves—stealing, cursing, flipping the ever-popular middle finger, and my least favorite, instigating fights. Their speech was filled with nonsense like "What up?" and "Yo!" and they all loved musicians with names like Snoop Dogg or Warren G.

Yes, hip-hop had arrived at my middle school.

The funny thing about hip-hop was I *liked* it! The beats, the clever rhymes, the fashion sense: It was dumb, but fun. Maybe being like everyone else wasn't a crime. I started thinking if the world had already gone to the "dawgs," then I might as well join them. I thought that if I listened to this music enough to memorize it, then I wouldn't get beat up or rejected from the different cliques.

5. **Entering the O-Zone**

As confused and scared as I was, I decided to act stupid (or "stoopid") like everyone else. I started using "street" language, cursing in every sentence, lacing my talk with double negatives, wearing flags in my back pocket, and "flipping the bird" at everyone.

I didn't have to fake the hip-hop limp to the side, because I have cerebral palsy. My new hip-hop friends didn't know that was the real way I walked, and they gave me respect for being a thug. I knew it was stupid, but after the abuse I'd taken, I was greedy for the attention and popularity.

> **After the abuse I'd taken, I was greedy for the attention and popularity.**

The Otis that everyone remembered as a well-educated young man was replaced by a character called "O-Zone," a boy who liked nothing but rap. Looking back, I'm surprised that I never beat myself up for being like everyone else. I kept thinking, "Am I me or am I them?"

The truth is, rap music never spoke to me on a deep level. Nothing about the aggression of rap made me feel tough, because it all seemed to be about acting like everyone else. And the lyrics are idiotic: "My chain is so shiny," or "I got mad money."

There was one artist I did identify with, who went beyond the rap clichés: Eminem. When you listen to this guy, it's as if you're actually feeling his pain when he talks about his mother or his girlfriend. I knew he raised controversy, but at the time most of what he was saying made sense to me, and that's more than you could say about other famous rappers.

6. **Blood Is Metal**

After three shameful years of junior high, I successfully moved on to high school. None of my old friends went there, so once again I had a chance to reinvent myself—and leave hip-hop behind. I went back to rock music and once again everyone picked on me because I wasn't like them.

> **Hard rock and metal help me control my anger by entering into it.**

I turned to one song in particular after I'd get beaten up—"Happy?" by Mudvayne. The sound was heavy enough to make you feel as though you were in a mosh pit and everyone was free to go as crazy as they wanted to. The singer, Chad Gray (or Kud), screams out lyrics about ripping wounds and tearing bones and then asks, "Are you feeling happy now?" That's the track I'd blare through my headphones after getting my ass handed to me.

Eventually, Mudvayne brought me more than lonely comfort. During lunch, I would hang out in the art room with my 9th grade art teacher, Ms. Fletcher, and write down the lyrics of rock songs in a notebook I carried. Four other 10th grade boys hung out there, too, and I'd listen to them talk. One day, the guy named Yusef said to one of his friends, Frankie: "Hey, did you hear Mudvayne's new album? They took the face paint off."

I interrupted, with a bit of hesitation, "I had no idea they made a new album—but they took the face paint off before, in their video for 'World So Cold.'"

7. **The Uses of Music**

I joined the conversation and soon I was part of the group. Yusef and the other guys turned my attention to metal bands like Celtic Frost, Slayer, Metallica, All That Remains, and Into

Eternity. Songs like "Severe Emotional Distress" by Into Eternity capture a feeling of emptiness that I find comforting.

Hard rock and metal help me control my anger by entering into it. The sound pulses through my veins and I picture myself in a music video for that particular song. In that video, nobody bothers me. The isolation doesn't feel lonely but great, like I have time to myself, and I'm as happy as I've ever been in my life.

As for Yusef and the rest of the guys, music brought us together as a group. We like discussing the musicians and the music, and it helps us talk about the personal stuff we go through.

Music can describe my mood, give me hope, and set me free from my encounters with bullies and thugs or even parents and siblings. It lets me share in someone else's emotions without revealing myself.

Otis was 18 when he wrote this story. He later graduated from high school and enrolled in Medgar Evers College.

Gay in Da Hood

By Jeremiyah Spears

1. Because I'm 6'6" and hefty, people often think I should be
a ball player of some sort. But once you get to know me,
you'll know I'm no ball player.

In my old neighborhood, guys would always call me out of
my house to play basketball, knowing that was not what I liked
to do. When I missed a shot they would ridicule me and call me
a f-ggot.

It's true, I'm gay, and though I look like your ordinary clean-
cut Polo boy, I act a little feminine. When I'm happy, I like to buy
shoes. I also like to read romances and family-oriented books. My
favorite book is *Mama*, by Terry McMillan. It's about a divorced
black woman with five kids who's having problems being accepted into society.

2. **Different From Day One**

In fact, I've been different my whole life. I first realized I was homosexual at an early age, because when I was around 5 or 6 years old, I would see boys and think, "How cute." Besides, I was labeled as different by many people. I never liked to play ball or get sweaty. My favorite toy was Christmastime Barbie. When the boys used to ruffhouz and try to do it to me, I'd tell them to leave me alone. I would never do any typical boy stuff, such as sports, play fighting, or rapping.

I could never understand why anyone would want to harass me for that. I used to think, "So what if I'm gay? So what if I'm different? Accept me or don't accept me at all, honey, because I'm just me." I couldn't understand why the boys wanted to bother me and fight me when they didn't know a damn thing about me. But they did.

> **I thought these guys would never understand me. They wanted to change me. They wanted to make me someone I wasn't.**

The boys in my neighborhood were rough-necked, ball-playing, weed-smoking boys who picked on people to prove their machismo to their friends. I think those boys did what they did because of their own insecurities, because they wanted to prove they were manly men.

3. **Halloween Humiliation**

There were about nine or 10 of them and they lived in or around my neighborhood. Wherever I went I always ran into them, and often they would torture me for being gay. One Halloween night, 1 went alone to catch the bus to go to a party. I was wearing a pair of dark jeans and a matching jacket and a black sweater with my initials on it. My mother had spent a lot for the outfit. She had spent $132 on the jacket alone.

While I was walking toward the bus, I saw a group of boys on bikes passing by. I recognized some of the guys. The first thought

I had was, "Oh no, they're going to start trouble with me." I kept walking.

All of a sudden a partially opened bottle of urine hit me and got all over me. Some straight guys think doing something like that to a gay guy is kind of creative. They all hurried away and I screamed and cried because of all the money my mom spent on the outfit.

Then I felt the same as always—puzzled as to why I had to be their victim. I thought these guys would never understand me. They wanted to change me. They wanted to make me someone I wasn't.

4. I Got Revenge

For three weeks after Halloween, I had the incident on my mind. At first my brothers were trying to get me to let them beat the boys up. But I thought that would not make the situation better. It would probably just wild up the problem more.

Finally I decided that I'd show them I wouldn't stand for it anymore and I began to fight—with my pen. I wrote them gruesome letters with fake blood (ketchup) smeared on to let them know I was going to get them back and that I'd get the last laugh. Ha!

Usually, when the guys harassed me, I would say, "F--- you," and "Go straight to hell, because I'm going to be me and there will be no changes until I feel that my life needs a change." And I would get revenge. I would make fun of them trying to talk to girls and getting turned down. Sometimes we'd end up fighting.

5. Never Any Peace

When we fought, often my brothers or my female friends would be there to help me—some of my female friends were known for beating guys down. And once I even whacked a guy with a plank. While I was fighting, I'd think blood and more blood, because of the traumatic experiences I'd been through. I wanted so much revenge on the boys who created trouble for me. Because of the fights, the cops were always at my house.

Even though it made me feel better for a short while to get revenge, I felt as if I was never going to succeed in having peace of mind. And after the fights were all over, I wouldn't feel much better. Often I felt as if I'd never belonged, and that no one would ever socialize with me because I was gay. I thought the world was so against me and that no one cared.

6. **Props From Friends**

Still, there were people around who helped me and supported me, like my brothers and my friends. Looking back, I can see how much of a difference they made, even when times were at their hardest.

When I was living in my old neighborhood, my best friend was Lauryne. Beauty was her name, and we would go to the movies, the mall, or just hang in the park and talk about everything, from boys and love to clothes, shoes, and jewelry.

> **Despite all the hassles I went through, the people who supported me made me feel that I didn't have to change myself for anyone.**

Sometimes we would cut school for days at a time, but we always got good grades in everything we did except for physical education, in which we had to beg for good grades, because we never showed up.

Like a lot of my other girl friends, Lauryne didn't really care that I was gay. As a matter of fact, she praised me for having the nerve to be able to come out at an early age to my parents and siblings and not really worry what they were going to think of me. She said things like, "You're brave," "You're courageous," and that she was lucky to have a friend like me.

It made me feel wonderful to know I had friends who honestly cared about me. It made me strong and gave me courage to be even more open about my sexuality, and to encourage other kids to come into the light and pay the price. It made me believe there would always be people to support me.

7. **My Grandma Taught Me the Golden Rule**

Another person who really helped me survive everything was my grandma, who raised me. From my grandma I learned strength, courage, patience, love, compassion, and to treat all people the same. My grandma taught me to learn new things from people who try to reach out and teach you. She taught me the golden rule: Do unto others as you want others to do unto you.

My grandma was born in 1919. She grew up on a farm and was born in a time when blacks weren't accepted and women weren't allowed to vote. She saw so much—the

> **My grandma had a strong sense of herself, and that made her open-minded.**

Great Depression, both World Wars, prohibition, segregation, lynchings, the civil rights movement. She would tell me about the marches, about the violence, and how once when she was in Jackson, Mississippi, she saw two boys who'd been hung from a tree.

She told me, "My dear, you haven't seen the harshness life can give you."

Sometimes people who have lived through hard times grow closed and mean and bigoted against people who are different from them. But my grandma had a strong sense of herself, and that made her open-minded to the different things in life. She always said, "People must know themselves before they try to learn from another person," and that's exactly what she did.

8. **'Don't Let No One Turn You Around'**

As for my grandmother trying to change me, like so many other people in the world have seemed to want to, it never happened. Instead, she encouraged me to do what I thought was right and what would make me happy. My grandma often told me that she'd always love me no matter who I was.

Real Men

Three months after I came into foster care, when I was no longer living with my grandma because she was ill, I received a call from my aunt saying my grandma wanted to speak to me. When she got on the phone, she said, "I love you dear, and don't let no one turn you around." Then she hung up the phone because she had gotten short-winded. Shortly after that conversation, she died. I love her dearly and I miss her.

I now live in a group home in a different part of the city. As for the boys in my neighborhood, they no longer bother me, because I don't go around there very often. When I do think back on things, sometimes I can laugh, but other times I'm still angry that those nobodies had so much control over my life.

Still, I think I have come to be OK being myself every day. Despite all the hassles I went through, the people who supported me made me feel that I didn't have to change myself for anyone. I know that my life would only get harder trying to change for other people's satisfaction. I know that I just need to satisfy myself.

Jeremiyah was 17 when he wrote this story.

WHERE WE ARE, AND WHERE WE WANT TO GO

Chapter 4

Coping With Difficult Feelings

Clean and Kind of Sober

By Antwaun Garcia

1. When I was a kid, I noticed how family members picked up a cigarette whenever they felt stress or got mad. My mom would hand me her bogey (cigarette) and tell me to flush it down the toilet. One day, when I was 9, I closed the bathroom door and smoked it.

   I figured that if my parents saw me smoking they'd laugh, like parents do when they watch a little girl walk in high heels impersonating her mother. But soon I used cigarettes the same way my parents did—to feel better.

2. **Could Anyone Understand Me?**

   When I was 10, my life got stressful. My friend Ricky died in a fire, and I went into foster care, moving to my aunt's house in Queens, New York, because my mom was using drugs.

   When I couldn't read a book my aunt gave me, thought about

how my dad used to hit my mom, or wondered what my mom was doing on the streets, I couldn't wait to smoke a cigarette. Sometimes I even sneaked a little alcohol. At family parties my grandma let us try it, and it made me feel loose.

Then, when I was 13, my best friend Jarrel killed himself. After he died, I drank a bunch of Bacardi and sat out on my terrace crying, confused and lost, thinking about my friends' deaths, not being with my parents or brothers, and feeling isolated instead of loved.

> **Fighting, drinking, smoking, and writing were the only ways I knew of to deal with my emotions.**

I felt completely alone. I doubted anyone could understand me or all that I had gone through.

3. Weed Became My Escape

After Jarrel died, I wrote many poems about guilt, death, and anger. I found that writing helped me vent my emotions. But the next year, when I got to high school, my boys put me on to something even better: smoking weed. I loved it from the first.

We cut class, went to my boy's crib, and smoked about four blunts. I took a mean pull, and after the second pull I didn't want to pass it around.

In my first two years of high school, I cut class hundreds of times and had a 55 average. I liked smoking so much because I never thought about my past or my life when I was high. I just thought about food and what I was going to do when I got home.

4. Drinking and Smoking Alone

I smoked mostly by myself, because when I was smoking with my friends, I would come out with thoughts that I later regretted sharing. I didn't want my boys to know me too well. By 15, I was lighting up by myself in a park far from my neighborhood.

By 17, I was also drinking a lot, taking Bacardi or Hennessy to school in water bottles or drinking after school in a park. I felt lonely, frustrated, angry, and helpless.

I thought it best to drink alone so I didn't show anyone my sadness or get in trouble. When I drank I wanted to fight. If I had liqs in me, I didn't care who the dude was, I threw the hands. With every fight, the anger of my childhood ran through my body. I didn't like who I was, but fighting, drinking, smoking, and writing were the only ways I knew of to deal with my emotions.

5. 'Antwaun, Are You OK?'

Then, when I was 18, I met a girl in my high school. She was a Dominican mami, a natural beauty, intelligent, loved to laugh, and had a beautiful smile. We had two classes together and eventually started dating.

Together we went shopping, to movies and amusement parks, and on picnics. At night we would sit in a park and talk for hours, or bug out in hotels, ordering pizza and watching movies and having bugged-out pillow fights. We couldn't get enough of one another.

But my habits started to affect our relationship. Every time I drank, the anger I bottled in came out. On the phone, she would hear me breathing hard and ask, "Antwaun, are you OK?" I'd tell her about a fight I had, usually because I was smoking or drinking.

She realized that smoking and drinking brought out the demon in me, which we were both scared of. My girl would cry because she felt helpless to calm or console me, and I'd get mad at myself for putting her through pain.

6. 'Your Habits Or Me'

Finally one day she told me, "Antwaun, you know I love you, right?"

"Yes!" I replied.

"I love you so much that it hurts. So you have to choose—your habits or me."

I didn't know what to say but I was thinking, "Antwaun, you're losing someone important, and for what? Choose her before you lose her!" So I told her I would stop.

I never completely stopped drinking. (My girl sometimes drank, too, and we'd have a few drinks together.) But I made a major effort to keep my cups under control. Smoking I stopped completely, because I didn't need to escape my reality when I was with her.

As I let her get to know me, she helped me let out some of the feelings I kept inside. To help her understand why I was so angry, I told her about my past.

We talked for hours about each other's pasts, even though her past wasn't like mine. She listened to me, so I felt at ease coming out with everything. I learned how to talk about my feelings rather than hide from them.

7. 'It's OK to Cry'

Whenever I started to cry, she would tell me, "You don't have to tell me if you're not ready," because she knew I hated crying. I would hold my head back and cover my eyes, and she would hug me and say, "It's OK to cry. I'm here. Everything is fine."

Whatever I didn't tell her about myself, she read in the stories I wrote. She kept a book of all my articles and saved them next to her journal and baby pictures. I also kept writing down all my emotions to release that feeling of pressure from holding too much in.

With my girl's help, I became more focused in school and my life started to look clearer. I was good.

8. A Deep Depression

After two years, my girl became depressed due to family issues. Then she moved away, and we broke up. After that, I fell into a deep depression that lasted for months. I felt alone and lost. I had no clue of what I wanted to do in life.

I started drinking and smoking again, fell off in school, and didn't wash because I wanted to look like I felt: dirty and pathetic. I was always mad. I stopped writing and let my pain eat at me.

My cravings for fast food became real serious, too. Whenever I went to Micky D's I ordered up to $8 worth of food from the dollar menu. If I ordered Chinese food, I got an egg roll to go with every dish. I gained almost 20 pounds that February. Now I was depressed, confused, alone, failing school—and fat!

Gradually, I got disgusted with myself and tired of always being depressed. I was

> **Getting high all the time was not helping me to be at peace.**

walking around in small T-shirts with a gut that hung low. My clothes felt tight. I felt like Homer Simpson with waves and a $5 tee.

I started wondering, "How am I going to get over my depression? What direction am I heading in life?" I wasn't the man I wanted to be. Getting high all the time was not helping me to be at peace. Finally, I couldn't stand myself anymore. I knew I had to change.

9. **My Mojo Returns**

It helped when my ex and my mom called and reminded me of my good points. "You always had a presence when you entered a room," my ex told me. My mom said she thought of me as a determined guy who never let anyone stand in his way. I began to remember my good characteristics. I am a funny, determined, caring, real dude with a passion to write and a gift for making people smile.

I decided to test myself to see if I could stop smoking weed. I started slowly, going a day without smoking by keeping myself busy. I avoided the weed spots, went to school, the library, and home.

I would get the urge to smoke at night. My anger had always given me energy. Without it, I felt lifeless and exhausted sometimes, as if the life force had drained out of me. I almost felt like if I didn't smoke or drink, I wouldn't wake up and feel alive.

10. **Showers and Workouts**

But when I got the urge to drink, cry, or smoke, I took long, 45 minute showers. It's a good thing my aunt didn't have to pay the water bill! I also started taking care of myself, putting on my jewelry, which I'd left on the dresser when I was depressed, and slowing down my eating to three meals a day.

> **When I saw my brother again in November and he was smoking weed, I passed it up. When I turned it down, I felt powerful.**

I started a workout regimen—running up and down steps, doing push-ups and sit ups. I started to feel good physically. Seeing that I could take control of my life made my confidence grow. As I felt better, I started to keep busier and be more social. Each change made other changes happen. A year later, I'm still in the process of getting myself back.

11. **One Last Pull**

Now I keep myself on the move—running in the morning, going to work in the afternoon. On weekends I chill with friends who don't smoke or drink. I play basketball with my sister, and take my little cousins to the movies. I don't have time to be alone and drink and smoke and reminisce about painful things.

The last time I smoked weed was four months ago. I was at my brother's apartment in Harlem. We ordered Chinese food, and one of my boys brought over some video games. We passed around some weed and drank orange juice and vodka while playing and conversing about sports and music. I didn't turn down the weed, because it didn't seem like a big deal to smoke one time with friends.

But the next morning I felt physically sick. I was coughing

hard and spitting non-stop. That turned me off to smoking. Since then I haven't smoked weed at all.

When I saw my brother again in November and he was smoking weed, I passed it up. When I turned it down, I felt powerful. I knew I could overcome my addiction to smoking weed. I was strict with myself and I stopped.

12. Stronger and More in Control

Since then, I've also cut down on smoking cigarettes (to one or two a month) and I don't drink recklessly to deal with stress—just when I'm at a party or celebration.

Both my parents have bad lungs and livers and are perfect examples of what I don't want for myself. My father is sick and paralyzed on the left side of his face but he still smokes and drinks. Now I realize that my parents may have gotten addicted to smoking, using crack, and drinking the same way I started: to cope with feelings of loneliness, anger, and fear.

I can't say I won't have any more depressions, or that the urge to drink or smoke won't ever overtake me, because I don't know what life has in store. But I know I've made a big change. I feel more in control of myself than ever before.

Antwaun was 21 when he wrote this story.
He later became a manager at a major hardware retailer.

Letting It Out

By Ashunte Hunt

1. When I was 14, I was put in my first group home. I was facing many struggles at that time: I was still grieving for my parents, who had died when I was younger, and I was living with a stepmom who abused me. I also had to deal with bullying from my peers in middle school.

I was caught in a circle of abuse, where I'd get beat up in school, which led to me getting in trouble, and then I would go home and go through the beatings that my stepmom called "discipline." When I was put in the group home, I had to deal with a whole new situation all by myself, so I got really stressed out.

I had no way to express my feelings because I wouldn't talk to anybody. I didn't trust them. Not being able to express my feelings gave me no choice but to keep them bottled up inside, and the more I bottled up my feelings the more likely I was to explode. My anger kept rising and rising, and then I'd get into fights or vandalize property. I always had evil thoughts in my head.

2. **My Own Jekyll and Hyde**

I looked at the world as if everybody was against me. I hated everyone I didn't know, and I grew very skeptical around the people that I did know. And if I felt that I was being disrespected in any way I'd just flip out like I was crazy.

I was my own Jekyll and Hyde—in certain situations I could control myself, but when someone provoked me I felt powerless to stop myself from going off on them. The people that pushed me to snap were the people that bullied me, made fun of my cir-

> **I had no way to express my feelings because I wouldn't talk to anybody. I didn't trust them.**

cumstances, and tried to play me like I was soft like wet bread.

When I got mad in my group home, I turned into a demolition man and demolished anything I could. I demolished couches, chairs, walls (I punched them in), and my room. I also picked fights whenever people pushed my buttons.

3. **Out of Control**

One day in my group home the barber came through, and I decided to get my hair cut. As I was waiting for my turn, I went downstairs and started playing a pinball game on the computer.

One of my peers came downstairs to tell me that it was my turn to get my hair cut. He tried to get me to come upstairs and he turned off the computer screen. I turned it back on. I thought he was playing at first, so I didn't get mad or take it seriously.

He did it again and I turned it back on to continue playing my game. I started to get agitated. If my anger was a pot of water on the stove, it was just starting to bubble.

When he did it for the third time, I turned it back on and told him, "If you turn off the computer screen again I will hurt you!"

This time I was mad—the water was about to boil over.

Then he did it again, and that knocked the water out of the pot. I was in a rage, and we started fighting. We got a couple of hits in, then staff came to break it up.

4. **Something to Relate to**

I had so much anger in me at my group home that I didn't really want to deal with anything that anybody wanted me to do. But one day my favorite group home staff let me listen to some of his music—albums by Tupac and Eminem. When I listened to them, I felt this unique feeling that no other artists gave me.

When I listened to Tupac's music, I got the message of street life and family problems. When I listened to Eminem's music, I felt the anger and rage that I'd been through. That's when the next stage opened up for me to walk on.

I was listening to Eminem when one song caught my attention. It was titled "Rock Bottom," and the song was about how life can really push you to the edge and bring you down.

The first line pulled me in: "I feel like I'm walkin' a tightrope without a circus net." And I related to that line because the lifestyle that I was going through made me feel like I was walking that tightrope. So I decided to write something of my own and I got a piece of paper and a pencil.

5. **Putting My Feelings on Paper**

In that first poem, I expressed my built-up anger, rage, and depression. I didn't feel anything while I wrote it. But a week later, I caught the feelings after reading it over and over again.

I called my first poem "Will somebody referee this fight I'm fighting?" One of the lines was: "I wouldn't care if the grim reaper reap, cause my life is something that I now don't want to keep." And that line alone hit me so hard that I had to dig into myself and see what would make me write that, because I really didn't recall writing it. That's when I realized how much pain I was in and how much I needed to release all my stress.

So I started writing more poetry. The poems that I wrote in

my group home were about me, my anger, depression, stress, and any other thing that bothered me. When I wrote poetry it was like I could just write forever to express my feelings.

6. **Calming My Anger...**

The poetry affected my anger a little at a time. When I started to feel angry, I'd write a poem or two to release my feelings before I did something that I'd regret. I'd still be angry, but I could at least let some of it out before it got out of hand.

When I found out that my first love had cheated on me, I wanted to chop her head off. Her love was priceless and I felt she threw my heart in the trash. I was so angry that I had to release my anger or I would have ended up in jail. So the first thing I did was write two poems. Then, when I saw her, I was able to stay calm even though it still hurt.

When I read over my poems I can acknowledge my

> **Writing my feelings down on paper taught me how to look at the world differently.**

feelings, and that helps me think about what I can do to make the situation better. I ask myself how I can do something different to avoid getting physical or making myself a threat to anybody.

I didn't get into that many fights after I started writing poetry, but I really can't say that it put an end to the fighting, either. Sometimes I feel like going back to my old behaviors when I get mad, because I still have a lot of anger inside of me. Certain situations give me flashbacks of how I would react if I were the old me.

7. **...But Not Completely**

I will still fight someone for disrespecting the memory of my mother and father, or for threatening me or my space. But it's been four or five months since I had my last fight.

And the last time I demolished something was a year ago. I was angry at my ex-girlfriend because we got into an argument over the phone, and I demolished my bowling trophy and some things that she had given me. I'll only demolish something if I'm so upset that poetry can't help me.

Poetry can't help me get over the abuse I've been through or the fact that my parents are gone. I have to reach deep down inside to recover from those things, and even though poetry helps me get in touch with my inside, it doesn't cover those subjects. It might help numb it at times but it doesn't hit the spot like I want it to.

But writing my feelings down on paper taught me how to look at the world differently, and to rationalize to the best of my ability if I couldn't do anything to decrease my feelings at the time. My temper has calmed down, and I don't feel powerless over my behaviors anymore. I feel like a real human being who can civilize himself and can let himself cool off on his own.

Ashunte was 17 when he wrote this story. He later attended college and worked as a teacher's aide and a security guard.

Karate Killed the Monster Inside Me

By Robin Chan

1. I was fed up. From the time I was 4 years old, I was teased and pushed around by bullies on my way home from school because I was short and frail-looking. My family and I also got harassed by racist punks because we were the only Asian people living in a white neighborhood.

    These incidents grew the hate monster inside of me. Most days, I would come home from elementary school either angry or crying. My family and friends tried to comfort me, but I had been storing up the loads of anger inside me for too long. I thought I was going to explode.

2. ## 'My Hit List'

    When I was about 9, I found the answer to my problems. I decided to learn karate so I could break the faces of all the people on my "hit list" (anyone who had ever bullied me or my family).

I started nagging my parents about learning karate. They agreed because they wanted me to build up my self-esteem, learn some discipline, and have more self-confidence. All I wanted was to learn the quickest way to break someone's neck, but I didn't tell that to my parents.

I was about 10 years old when I finally got my chance. My first dojo (that's what martial arts students call the place where they study and practice) was small, musky, and smelled lightly of sweat. The instructor, Mr. Sloan, was as strict as an army drill sergeant.

> **I was teased and pushed around by bullies.**

Mr. Sloan taught us how to do strange abdominal exercises that were like upside down sit-ups and really difficult. He wouldn't allow any slacking off from people who got tired. It was only the first day—what did he want from us? I quickly discovered that I was really out of shape. Before the first lesson was over, I was already thinking about dropping out.

3. Learning Skills and Getting in Shape

By the end of the second lesson, however, I had decided to stick with it. Mr. Sloan was teaching us cool techniques for breaking out of arm and wrist locks and that got me interested.

Mr. Sloan was a good instructor. Within a few months, my class of beginners went from learning the basic punch, block, and kick, to learning a flying jump kick. He also taught us effective techniques for breaking out of headlocks and strangleholds. We enhanced our skills by sparring with each other and practicing at home.

Although the dojo had limited resources (there were no boards to break, no martial arts weapons, and no fighting gear), I still learned a lot and had a lot of fun. I became more flexible from the rigorous exercises. In addition to practicing our karate moves, we did push-ups, sit-ups, and leg, arm, torso, and back stretches to limber up. We also meditated together.

4. **Learning Respect**

Near the end of class, Mr. Sloan would guide us through the meditation by telling us to clear our minds. One time, he told us to picture ourselves breaking free of a barrier or knocking a barrel or a wall to pieces. He said that whenever we had problems or faced challenges that got us frustrated, we should go to a quiet place, relax, and close our eyes. In our minds, we should picture ourselves knocking over that problem or challenge. Mr. Sloan said that doing this should make us feel better. After meditating on "killing" the problem, he said, our minds would be clear and we'd be more determined to solve it.

Mr. Sloan also made it clear that he was teaching us karate not just so we'd be able to kick someone's ass real good, but so each of us could become a role model. A role model, he explained, was someone with a good conscience, good morals, self-respect, and respect for others.

We worked on developing these qualities in class by bowing to the instructor, addressing him as "sir" or "sensei," treating fellow students with respect, and listening to our sensei's lectures, which taught us about respect, discipline, manners, and so on. We were taught to exercise these qualities not only in the dojo, but outside as well.

> **I knew that I was now capable of protecting myself against enemies. Whether I chose to fight was beside the point.**

The goal of becoming a role model was a major factor in my wanting to continue to study karate. I no longer saw the martial arts as a way to get back at people who hurt me. I knew from experience that there were enough menacing and evil people in this world. I didn't want to become one of them.

5. ## Discipline Helped Me Stay in Control

After a few months, I was much more self-confident and disciplined. I knew that I was now capable of protecting myself against enemies. Whether I chose to fight someone who bullied me was beside the point; I knew that I could knock them out. Just knowing that made me feel good about myself, so why fight when you're already ahead? Besides, not fighting would save my knuckles from a lot of pain.

The insults and slurs I encountered did not bother me as much anymore. As a matter of fact, the discipline and basic philosophy I learned from karate held back the punches I was tempted to throw when people tried to provoke me to fight.

For example, one day when I was walking home from school, two teenaged guys walked into me. One of them said, "Watch it, ch-nk" and shoved me. They started pushing me but I just blocked their pathetic pushes. They weren't getting enough thrills from just shoving me, so they started cursing and spitting at me too.

6. ## I Didn't Need to Fight

I started getting really aggravated. Then I remembered something Mr. Sloan had told me when I asked him what to do when someone bothers you. "Low-lifes like these do not deserve the time and energy you put into punching them out," he said. "Just walk away and splash some cold water on your face."

I cooled down and started walking away. The two guys saw that I was not affected by their stupid remarks. I heard one of them say, "Forget that ch-nk, man."

It was ironic how I wanted to learn karate so that I could beat up people like these, and then, when I got the chance, I didn't go through with it. What karate taught me was that fighting isn't the right way to solve a problem. It just turns you into one of those low-lifes who don't have the conscience, respect, manners, or education to know how to handle their problems any other way.

I was good enough at karate by that point that it wouldn't have been a fair fight. But if I had given in to the temptation to beat those guys up, I would have felt ashamed and guilty. I would have disappointed Mr. Sloan, who taught me that the most important rule of karate is not to fight unless it's necessary for self-defense; my parents, who told me never to fight with anyone even if they are wrong; and myself, because I feel that it is wrong to take advantage of a situation.

7. **Becoming a Role Model**

The time and effort I was putting into karate was getting me worthwhile results. I used to be wild when I was with my friends, but I had become more reserved and well-behaved. I also used to slack off in school but not anymore. I really started gearing up and hitting the books. My teachers and parents noticed the difference and were happy with what they saw.

I was even becoming a role model for some of my friends. They told me that they had never seen me work so hard before, and they admired the high grades I was earning in school. They decided to follow my example and started pulling their acts together and improving their own grades.

> **The discipline and basic philosophy I learned from karate held back the punches I was tempted to throw.**

Unfortunately, Mr. Sloan's class ran for only a year and when time was up, all of us were really upset. But our instructor had a new class of misfits to turn into the fine role models we had become.

Studying karate was a wonderful experience. I'm thankful to my extraordinary instructor, Mr. Sloan, and to my great family who let me go to the dojo and have supported me always. Together, Mr. Sloan and my parents have made me realize that I should always try my best and put a sincere effort into whatever I do. They have geared me up, morally and spiritually, to reach for the stars.

Robin wrote this story when he was 16. He later went to college and graduate school, and became a flight surgeon in the U.S. Air Force. He served in Afghanistan.

Don't Keep It Inside: Talk It Out

By Norman B.

1. In the past four years, I've had four different therapists. Each time I went to one I was hoping to find someone who cared enough to help me identify the things I did wrong and help me go about changing them. But until I found my fourth therapist, I was lost inside my own world.

   I went to my first therapist at age 12. At the time, my life was filled with chaos, and I didn't know who to talk to or how to handle it. My dad was in jail, my mother and I weren't talking, and in a little more than a year several family members had died. All the feelings I had began to build up inside, and I felt like I was drowning in my emotions.

2. **Acting Out**

   Sometimes I would cry like a baby over all the death in my family. Other times I'd feel angry and confused. I didn't trust anyone, especially my family, and I thought people were saying negative things about me. I started to disrespect my elders, steal, stay out late, and fail in school.

Things got so bad that I was sent to two different group homes. At the homes I pretended to feel better about myself, but being there made me feel like more of a failure and like I didn't deserve to live. I really needed someone to talk to. I needed someone to show me that there was still hope for me and to help me realize that everything that was going on wasn't all my fault.

> **I didn't trust anyone, especially my family.**

I went to one therapist after another. But my therapists didn't ask how I was really feeling, which was what I wanted. Instead they just skimmed the surface of the problems and offered me dumb advice like "Watch your temper," or "Try to fit in."

3. **Pretending It Didn't Hurt**

But my fourth therapist, Dr. Kaputer, was different. She didn't talk to me like I was a toddler. And she hardly ever talked about herself. She didn't act like I had to take her advice just because she went to school for it. And if I ever forgot to come for an appointment, she'd call to remind me. That alone made me feel like she really cared. Slowly I began to open up and tell her more about myself.

I remember one time I was hit in the face by another resident of my group home, and it left a mark under my eye. From that day until the mark went away, I was picked on. It was like I was garbage in a dumpster, and the residents were the seagulls—just picking and picking at me until there was practically nothing left.

I pretended that what they said didn't hurt, but it did. They would say things like "Norm's a punk," or "Check out big Norm with the black eye." Even though it was a joke to them, it wasn't to me.

4. **Opening Up**

At first I didn't want to talk to Dr. K about the fight too much. I didn't care how it started, or the consequences I had to suffer. It was the reactions I got from people that bothered me, and that was what I wanted to talk about.

She asked me how I felt about all the attention I was getting. Of course I said I was angry and didn't like it. But then she repeated the question, explaining that she wanted to know how I really felt about people making fun of me.

Again I tried to work my way around the question, but I didn't get far because she asked again. Finally, I told her, "It hurts so bad until I can't describe it," which is what she wanted to hear—and what I needed to say. How I really felt. After that session, it became easier for me to express my true feelings.

5. **Feelings Build Up**

Another time someone spread a rumor saying that I had sex with one of the residents. That whole thing went around the entire campus infecting people's brains like crack. And it lasted for weeks. Some of the residents would say, "Your roommate said you had sex with another resident," or "Yo, I heard you was gay, is that true?"

> **I made myself go completely numb to the hurt, only feeling anger. But it didn't work.**

To me, that was hurtful and embarrassing. I felt like I wanted to die, but I never let anyone know how I was really feeling. I just made myself go completely numb to the hurt, only feeling anger. But it didn't work because all my other feelings continued to build up, colliding and swarming around like the winds of an unpredictable storm.

I was rude to the other residents for the littlest things. Like when one asked if he could have some of my cereal, I said, "No, what the hell do I look like giving you something of mine, anyway?" He just rolled his eyes and walked away.

Another resident asked if I had a bar of soap he could borrow. I responded, "Do I look like your freakin' mother to you?" He just started mumbling and walked away, as well.

My anger was a reflection of how much I was hurting inside. Because I was hurting so badly and didn't want anyone to know, I became more and more angry, and that's when Dr. K really got down to business.

6. **Going Deeper**

Dr. K told me she thought I was trying to get at people's most sensitive, vulnerable sides, so I could make them feel the way I felt. Then she began to dig deeper. Instead of just telling me not to act out anymore, she asked me why I did it. How did it make me feel to insult someone? Did I think it was a positive thing to do?

> **With Dr. K's help, I realized that the ways I was acting were just a cover for my true feelings.**

At first I didn't know what to say to her questions because they were so direct. I explained to her that the things they said about me really hurt. And it wasn't just the fact that they weren't true. It was the fact that some of the same people saying these things claimed to be my friends.

But I also liked that she was willing to be so direct with me. With questions like that, I knew we were getting somewhere and that I was dealing with someone who cared. Which is what I wanted all along—someone who was going to be there for me. Someone who understood both sides of the story.

Working with Dr. K, I learned not to get so angry at so many little things. She helped me uncover a side of myself I never knew I had and showed me how to look at myself from the outside in. With her help, I realized that the ways I was acting were just a cover for my true feelings.

7. **A Reason to Live**

I still have to work on expressing my feelings more and not always thinking someone is talking bad about me. I still have to work on watching the things I say or at least how I say them. Which may take a while.

But Dr. K also helped me see that the things that went on at my group home weren't all my fault, and what was my fault I'd have to admit to. And she helped me realize that I actually did have a reason to live.

Dr. K helped me beyond words. She was the only person I trusted. So it really hurt me the day I found out she was leaving. I just felt like shutting out everything around me.

It's going to be hard to start with another therapist because I don't feel like going back and talking about my past after doing it with four other therapists. I just want to move forward. I just need someone I feel I can trust, with whom I can really talk about myself and my life. Sometimes, I just need to talk about me. Just me.

Norman was 16 when he wrote this story.

Chapter 5

Getting an Education

Will the Tortoise Win the Race?

By Eric Green

1. Everybody says you need to graduate from high school to succeed in life. But what if you just can't pass your classes? Should you keep trying? I'm 20 years old and I'm still in the 11th grade. I failed 9th grade once and failed 10th grade three times. I'm not sure I'll ever graduate.

Until 9th grade, I was in special education classes. In elementary school, I felt like the smartest kid in the class. I was a straight A student. In junior high, I constantly got 100s on spelling quizzes, and sometimes made the honor roll.

But it was back in 6th grade that I started to have trouble for the first time. When my math teacher called me up to the board to solve a problem, I was the slowest one to finish in the whole class. Some of my teachers yelled and screamed at me. One teacher called me "slow" and "stupid." I began to hate her and think of myself as stupid. On good days, I'd tell myself, "I'm smart, just not as quick as other people."

2. **'I'm Not Slow'**

In the 9th grade, I got switched to regular classes and went to the resource room for extra help. In my regular classes, students talked down to kids in special ed, calling us slow. I'd think, "That's where you're wrong. I go to the resource room because I have a learning disability, and I'm willing to get as much help as possible." But I kept my mouth shut because I didn't want to get teased even more.

That year, my biological mom died. My mind was not on school at all. Suddenly school was too hard. I seemed to have lost my ability to understand the work. I began to think I was not intelligent enough to pass high school classes. I would sit in class looking at the assignment while everyone else completed theirs.

> **On good days, I'd tell myself, "I'm smart, just not as quick as other people."**

Sometimes when I took an assignment seriously I'd do well. Then I'd feel proud and confident. Most of the time, though, I'd become overwhelmed and frustrated.

3. **I Tried My Hardest**

Once, in math class, I got extra help and did all of my assignments. When I got my report card, I saw that my math teacher had given me a 65.

"Why did you give me a 65?" I asked him.

"You didn't do well on the exams," he said.

I was furious. Didn't he know I was working as hard as I could? Didn't he understand how it feels to try hard but not be rewarded or recognized? I thought I deserved a better grade because of my effort, even if I couldn't do well on the tests.

4. **I'll Never Catch Up**

Situations like that made me feel neglected by my teachers. Growing up, my parents and my first foster parent neglected me.

My biological parents would disappear without a trace and leave my siblings and me in the house for hours. They didn't seem to notice who I was or what I needed.

I felt the same way when my teachers overlooked the efforts I made, or stood by while other kids in the class teased me and called me names. I felt that some of my teachers did not want to deal with me anymore and didn't pay attention to me when I asked for help. I felt lonely and isolated and stuck with problems that I couldn't solve.

> **I hoped that my teachers would notice that I was angry, or lost. But they only seemed frustrated.**

Eventually, I stopped asking for help. I'd feel stupid any time I tried to complete a difficult task. I stopped believing that I could ever pass, even if I got all the extra help in the world. I thought I'd never be a successful person.

Then I began to refuse to do class work. I'd spend my time writing poems or drawing pictures—two things I know I'm good at. When the teacher asked me about the assignment I was supposed to be doing, I'd have nothing to show.

5. 'Inattentive' and 'Uncooperative'

I hoped that my teachers would notice that I was angry, or lost. But when I took my adoptive mother, Lorine, to my parent-teacher conferences, my teachers only seemed frustrated.

One teacher told her, "Eric is a very talented poet and artist, but he doesn't do the work that is required of him. He just sits in the back of the classroom and writes his poems. He is very inattentive and uncooperative. He's a nice young man. I know he can do better."

Lorine said, "You see, that's the same exact thing that I be telling him. He gets mad and starts to cop an attitude. He doesn't like to study, or do his homework. Every day he just comes home and sits on the floor and draws and writes poems."

Every teacher we met told my mother the same thing. Even my art teacher, whose class is my favorite, told her, "Eric is not paying attention in class; he does not do the assignments. Eric does what he wants to do."

6. **'School Won't Help Me'**

I felt embarrassed because it was the truth. I knew that I should do what was asked of me instead of being troublesome. But when Lorine asked me why I wouldn't cooperate with my teachers, I was too embarrassed to come out with the reason for my behavior—that I felt like a failure. So I said, "I believe that school should suit my interests. I don't understand how learning math will help me become a poet or an artist!"

> **Some days I feel smart and hopeful, other days I'm discouraged.**

Finally, the anxiety and the feeling of wasting my life got to be too much. I told my mother, "I am dropping out."

"If you decide to drop out of high school, then you can leave this house and live with someone else," Lorine said.

7. **A New School**

Luckily, my counselor helped me transfer to a smaller high school where I could get more attention. I thought that in a better environment I would do better in school and be able to go forward in life. At first, I was more focused and willing to do the work. The teachers went out of their way to help me, and the students were respectful and easy to get along with.

My counselor also explained to me that having a learning disability is different from being dumb. "When you're a smart person with a learning disability, you can master an academic curriculum if you have plenty of assistance and you work hard. A dumb person is one who is unwilling to participate in classes or stick to the curriculum," she said.

Lately, though, I've run into some new obstacles. In New

York, you have to pass certain exams to graduate. I've taken some of those exams—in history and English—and I've failed all of them, some more than once. That made me feel depressed. I feared that I might never be a normal student and might never graduate from high school.

8. **Not Sure What to Believe**

When I confided in some of my teachers, they told me, "You need to have confidence in your abilities. You have potential and the intelligence to succeed. You're smart, creative, artistic, and unique. You write beautiful poetry. Believe in yourself."

Right now, I'm not sure what to believe about myself. Some days I feel smart and hopeful, other days I'm discouraged. On those days, I don't even try to work toward graduation. I just sit in my classes, drawing and writing poetry. Those are my talents, and when I look at the words and pictures I've created, I feel like it doesn't matter if I succeed in high school or not.

Still, if I don't graduate, I'll feel like a fool for letting myself and my family and friends down. I'm a smart person, I want to succeed, and everybody's in my corner. My friends tell me, "Your mother is right to be upset with you. You need an education." My mom tells me, "I want to see you with that paper in your hand."

I want to see that, too.

Eric was 21 when he wrote this story. He succeeded in graduating from high school later that year.

No More Hand-Holding

By Edgar Lopez

1. I sat in the back of the bus next to my friend Kevin. We were on our way to Philadelphia to visit colleges with our 8th grade class, and I was happy to be away from school for the next four days. When girls sat down next to us to wait for the bathroom, I went with the old-fashioned move: the yawn and act like I'm stretching to put my arm around them. "When are we gonna go out, baby?" I asked one girl.

   The main purpose of the trip was to give us a taste of college life and introduce us to college professors and students. But for us students, the real purpose was to escape from school and parents, and to have fun during the long bus rides and in the hotels. Or so I thought.

2. **Heard It All Before**

   We arrived at Lincoln University in Pennsylvania, our first

destination, around noon. It looked like a fun place to be. Students were studying on the lawns and hanging out with their friends. I noticed some were still wearing pajamas, or shorts and flip-flops. I pointed out to one of my teachers that a successful educational institution did not have to require uniforms like ours did. She just smiled and shook her head.

After lunch we went outside to talk with a group of college students. I was in the back, playing around with my friends and half paying attention. "Not another boring talk," I thought.

Everything the students said, I had heard before: "College is fun but you have to balance your school life and social life," and, "All you do in college is read, so be prepared for it."

3. **Hearing Something New—and Scary**

When my classmate Sandra (not her real name) raised her hand, I shook my head. She loved to show off her vocabulary. "What was the most perplexing experience you faced in the transition from high school to college?" she asked.

"I think having the freedom is a problem, because if you aren't serious it becomes very easy to fail," said one of the college students. That wouldn't be a problem for me, I thought. I knew how to stay focused.

> **I decided I needed to start working more independently now, so that I'd be ready for college.**

"Having to buy all your textbooks is the hardest part," answered a tall Hispanic student. I knew about having to purchase your own materials, so that wasn't a shock either.

My teacher's nephew Michael, an African-American freshman, was next. "The hardest thing for me was not having teachers who were close to me. I went to a small school in Manhattan like you guys, where all the teachers were supportive and gave students that extra push to succeed. They don't do that here. All they want is their tuition money," he said.

Suddenly, I was like, "Whoa." He seemed just like us—a young male from Brooklyn. That connection allowed me to see for the first time the situation I might face in a few years. And it terrified me.

My school, which I've attended since 6th grade, is small and all the students and teachers know each other well. I was a decent student but I was lazy and held my work on cruise control. My teachers often pushed me to do better and offered a lot of extra help. I'd grown accustomed to that nurturing and expected it to continue as I got older.

> **I knew I wasn't achieving my goal of self-reliance, but slacking off was like an addiction.**

Hearing how different college would be from someone with an experience similar to mine made me scared I might be unsuccessful there. I didn't know how to get things done without that extra push from teachers. I looked around and saw no one else moved by his words. Was I the only one who got the message?

4. **How Can I Change?**

Three days later, the long bus ride home gave me a chance to reflect on my fear. I decided I needed to start working more independently now, so that by the time college came around, I'd be ready. But who was going to help me get to a point of self-reliance? Because ironically, I knew I could not become self-reliant alone. I felt I needed to slowly experience independence and grow accustomed to it.

I decided to go to the root of the problem, which was my dependence on a particular teacher in our school, Ms. Stevenson. She was a good teacher and students could talk to her about anything. I decided I had to ask her if she could help me become more independent.

5. **'I Need Your Help'**

Two days after we returned from the trip, I nervously walked down the stairs toward Ms. Stevenson's office. I didn't want my request to backfire and have one of my most supportive teachers no longer be there for me. Or, even worse, she might think I was ungrateful for all her help.

"Ms. Stevenson, may I please speak to you?" I said, standing in the doorway of her office.

"Sure Edgar, what's wrong?" she said.

I started out by telling her what the college students had told us on the trip. Then I told her, "Ms. Stevenson, I need to learn how to approach problems with my schoolwork on my own. I really appreciate all the help you give me, but if I don't get used to doing stuff on my own now, by the time college comes around I'm going to be in trouble," I said.

> **I needed to slowly experience independence and grow accustomed to it.**

I was relieved when she said, "I understand and I'm glad you've decided to do this." Later that day, we met and made a plan.

6. **The First Plan Fails**

Her first idea was to stop checking on me. Ms. Stevenson would often come by my class and give me a mad look if she saw me playing around. I knew that look meant "get to work," and I counted on it to get focused.

We agreed that if she no longer did that, it would force me to get serious on my own, for my own benefit. We also agreed that I would stop going to her for help with schoolwork unless I made an extra effort on my own first.

It was a good plan. Unfortunately, it didn't work. Right away, I took advantage of our deal and became more of a slacker than ever. I walked around in the hallway during class because I knew Ms. Stevenson wouldn't be checking on me. I knew I wasn't achieving my goal of self-reliance, but slacking off was like an addiction. Besides, I was confident I could perform on the tests, so my grades would be fine.

7. **Nobody Changes Overnight**

Then my report card arrived in June. My average had plummeted about 10 points for the first time ever. I felt horrible. It made me feel that I couldn't do this alone, and I felt even less confident in my ability to perform in college. But I told myself that nobody just changes overnight. I had to keep trying.

"You're back," Ms. Stevenson said when I appeared in her office again.

> **Instead of complaining that I didn't know a topic, I began to read more about it.**

"Yeah, have you seen my report card?" I said.

"I knew this would happen. Do you see what I've been trying to keep you away from?"

That report card turned out to be a good reality check. Now I knew what would happen if I wasn't self-reliant. I needed to get serious about becoming a more independent student.

8. **On My Own**

Over the next year, my freshman year in high school, there were many more obstacles on my path to self-reliance. I failed biology my first semester and did poorly in math.

But all the work I handed in was mine alone. It felt good that I wasn't going to Ms. Stevenson for help. After I did badly that first semester, I decided to cut out the baby in me and do what I needed to do to improve my grades.

I developed a study schedule. Every day I devoted no less than 30 minutes to every subject I received homework for, instead of not studying at all, like before. Instead of complaining that I didn't know a topic, I began to read more about it.

And instead of spending money on expensive sneakers or

clothes, I invested in myself. I went to Barnes & Noble and found biology textbooks that targeted high school graduation exams and went into more depth than my schoolbooks.

9. **Ready for College**

By the end of my freshman year, I realized I was working independently. My study habits were now a part of my routine. My greatest moment was seeing my report card that June.

I had done better in all of my classes. I was most excited to see an 85 for my French class, the hardest class I had. Through my own persistence I had improved my grade by 15 points.

Now I never expect anyone to hold my hand and do my work for me. I'm not a machine that knows everything, but I don't automatically run for help anymore when I can't comprehend something. This has helped me prepare for the real world, during college and after it.

Edgar wrote this story when he was 17.

Community College:
A Second Chance

By Jordan Temple

1.   I used to think community colleges were just a fall-back option
     if you completely bombed in high school. That's kind of what
happened to me, actually. I attended four different high schools
over four years, and I chose to clown around instead of doing my
work. I was a know-it-all with false confidence. I felt that because
of my strong grades in middle school and freshman year of high
school, I was in the clear to meander through the halls instead of
attending class.

I finally got my act together a year and a half ago at my fifth
high school, John V. Lindsay Wildcat Academy, a school that
helps kids catch up on their credits and improve their grades.
If it wasn't for that school, which pulled me in and helped me
graduate, I'd probably be in a dead-end job instead of pursuing
a career.

I knew that I wanted to go to college last year when I started getting my grades up. I felt better about myself and I had a good sense of what I should be doing—furthering my education. Over a year and a half, I worked to earn credits and improve my grades at Wildcat Academy. Finally, last January, I graduated high school.

2. **Not Just a Fallback**

When my guidance counselor suggested I look through the SUNY (State University of New York) handbook to see which two-year colleges I might like to attend, I felt regretful that I didn't have the grades to go to a four-year college.

But I was glad I could attend college, period. I figured that if I worked hard and managed my money I could transfer to a four-year college and leave with a bachelor's degree, accumulating less debt than I would have if I'd gone to a four-year college the whole time.

I was relieved when I found out that some SUNY community colleges had dorms, because I wanted to get out of New York City, meet new people, and get the entire college experience. I wanted fresh air and a change of scenery, away from the distractions of city life and friends.

> **I didn't have the grades to go to a four-year college. But I was glad I could attend college, period.**

I eventually settled on Onondaga Community College in Syracuse, one of the largest community colleges in central New York. There are 9,000 day students and 500 students who live in dormitories. The college's website and virtual tour of the dorms blew me away, and so did the quality of the professors.

3. **A Clean Slate**

I met professors at an open house and it made it that much easier for me to choose Onondaga over the three other community colleges that I was accepted to. I was interested in communications, and the teachers explained what courses would benefit me and what careers I could pursue with that major (like marketing, public relations, or teaching). Plus, my credits would easily transfer to a four-year college after two years.

When I first got there, I was really shy and kept to myself. But I grew to like living in the dorms and meeting people. Students were friendly. They held doors for each other from about 20 feet away, and said hello.

I also liked the academic scene. I felt like I'd been given a clean slate. Now I could become more of an individual instead of keeping up my slacker image.

4. Lessons in Communication

I took four classes my first semester: interpersonal communication, English, oceanography, and a class about college study habits. My professor for that class was stern but cool. He was a middle-aged African-American man whose Afrocentricity rivaled my mother's.

> **I found that the library is where I am most focused. I practically lived there my first semester.**

He had posters of Malcolm X in his office and wore dashikis (traditional African garb) to class. We spoke about my grades, what classes I enjoyed, my major, issues in the black community, and my favorite sport, baseball. It was nice to have a professor I could talk to.

I also found ways to have intercultural communication. I was interested in clubs that brought people together. At Onondaga, I found two that did just that. I joined the ESL mentoring program, where an American-born student is paired with an international student. You meet twice a week to share your cultures, opinions, and questions, and talk about college life.

I was paired with Seung Young Kim, a student from Korea. We talked about the difference between North and South Korea, Korean celebrities, and America's favorite pastime (and mine): baseball. We became good friends and learned a lot from each other.

5. **Living in the Library**

I also joined the JAAMA club, a club that promotes unity among African-Americans on campus and shares ideas about issues in the black community. In the fall, I'm going to run for student representative, which would mean I'd be responsible for getting money for the club at student government meetings and recruiting more people to join.

Most importantly, I figured out my study habits. I found that the library is where I am most focused. I practically lived there my first semester. My plan is to get my grades up and then transfer to a four-year college. Many Onondaga students transfer to Syracuse University after two years, and I hope that I can do the same.

Even if I don't get into Syracuse, I want to attend a four-year college that has a good speech communications program, a marketing and business program, and a center for aspiring entrepreneurs.

6. **I Know Who I Am**

One day I'd like to become a baseball scout and, eventually, general manager of a baseball team. I also want to start a non-profit to fund low-income kids to go to baseball camp. I want to start an initiative to get more blacks back in baseball—in front offices, on major league teams, playing abroad, scouting, and playing minor league ball. A background in business and marketing would help me with that.

But for now, my focus is school. This fall I hope to maintain a 3.3 GPA or higher. I also would like to be more outgoing and attend more school events, go to a party or two, and contribute to a poetry slam. I developed a passion for writing poems my first semester. I thought a lot at school, and I started wanting to write down my thoughts (in between essays and homework).

I'm glad I embraced the idea of community college even though I had my doubts about it at first. College has been a great experience so far. I feel a lot more at peace with myself now. I know who I am: a kid who loves to read and learn new things (and is obsessed with baseball). I can see the purpose in everything that I do now, and how doing well in the present will help solidify my future. Community college hasn't been a disappointment, but a second chance.

Jordan was 20 when he wrote this story.

Freshman Year Is a Fresh Start

By Ferentz Lafargue

1. To all you roosters and chickenheads clucking it up in those high school hallways, cutting class and doing all kinds of junk: I advise you to get your act together and find a way to get into college, because college is the bomb, the shiznik, the booyah joint, or as I now say, the Jello bath!

I can't front. When I started my first semester at Queens College, I was lost. I had just finished a subpar (at least I thought so) four years of high school. As a matter of fact, I was still checking my mailbox for the letter telling me that my graduation was an accident. I kept expecting that I was going to have to return my diploma and report back to high school.

Luckily, that never happened and I soon found out that college is very different from high school. Well, at least it can be if you want it to. First of all you get a fresh start. You don't have to walk into class and act like a clown or a hardhead.

2. Nobody Knows You

In high school, you have to do that because a lot of your friends from junior high are there and you want to impress them. But in college nobody knows you. They don't know that you're a clown, and if you are they don't care, because they're there to learn. You get to be yourself, because that's really all that's asked of you.

Well, you also have to do the work. The teachers—excuse me, professors—don't play around. If they do, you're in trouble, because remember you're the one who's paying for the classes.

> **In college nobody knows you. You get to be yourself.**

There are two types of college classes. First, there's the type like my English class that are practically discussion groups. You're given a book to read and all that is asked of you is to be able to analyze and discuss it.

Then there are the dreaded lecture courses, where you sit for two hours while the professor talks to her heart's content on any subject, while you take notes. These classes are usually held in rooms the size of an auditorium, and there are at least 200 people in them, so it's a mission just to get to a seat.

3. Strutting My Stuff

One of the best things about college, for me at least, is that doing the work is fun (most of the time). I've learned that if I do my best, something good will always come out of it. For example, one day during my English class something came over me and I just started blurting out literary terms—foils, juxtapositions, ironies. If it was in the story I found it. It was clear to everyone that I'd understood what I'd read.

A professor who'd been observing the class came by and told me how bright I was. After she finished praising me, my professor asked me if I'd be interested in a fellowship (like a scholarship) for English majors. It was after this conversation that I realized that I have a gift and it should be worked on.

I began taking my work more seriously, because success seemed closer. It wasn't like in high school. Back then I lacked the confidence to pursue awards, and when I did it was usually halfheartedly so that if I didn't get them I could always say, "Well, of course not, I didn't try."

4. **It's Not All Work**

And college isn't all work. Another important part is being able to make new friends, and if you can make them on your own terms it's even better. (Meaning that you're getting along with everyone and having fun while still keeping up with your work.)

In high school I was mad quiet (when I wasn't clowning around, that is) and it made people think that I was conceited. Kids were uncomfortable around me, because they thought I didn't like them. To be honest, I didn't go out of my way to make any friends, either. When I got into college I was determined to change this, so I followed this simple rule: "Open up and whoever wants to come in, will come in." And it works.

I'm having the time of my life in college. I'm even glad that I decided to stay at home instead of going away to school. When people come and tell me how much fun I could be having if I had gone away or gone to a bigger school, I don't care. Those people never mention how expensive dorms get to be, or the possibility of having the roommate from hell, or how pizza and take-out Chinese food tend to lose their appeal after awhile.

> **I began taking my work more seriously, because success seemed closer.**

5. **If I Could Just Get Some Sleep**

When you go to school in a big city, even if you're still living with your folks, there's never a dull moment. After school or work you can hop on a bus or train and go see a movie, get some Japanese food, or just go home and rest. If you think you're going to be missing out on something and want to pay your own bills and all that stuff, just tell your parents. They'll be more than happy to treat you like an adult for about $500 a month to cover room and board.

There is one thing that I've missed out on since starting college and that's sleep. In fact, the key to success in college is to sleep whenever and wherever you get a chance—because you won't get the chance too often.

Ferentz was 18 when he wrote this story. He later graduated from college, earned a PhD in African-American and American Studies from Yale, and became a college professor.

Chapter 6

Getting Money

It Wasn't Easy, But I Did It: How I Found My Job

By Sharif Berkeley

1. **I**t's one of those days when you have no money and each hour seems to melt away with you sitting on the couch. You see your friend who's just cashed his check from work. He's showing off because his pockets are full and you're feeling bad because you've only got lint in your pockets.

You finally say to yourself, "I need a job!" But then you think to yourself, "How do I go about getting one?"

Looking for a job can be one of the most tedious and frustrating events of life, especially for young people without any experience. But if you look in the right places and spread yourself around, a job is sure to come your way.

2. **You Can't Give Up**

A lot of people make up excuses about why they don't have a job. The most popular is, "I went looking already and I can't find one." People who say this will just continue being unemployed until they wake up.

Looking for a job is something that you can't give up on, because if you do you'll be right back to square one with five balls of lint and a rubberband in your pocket instead of money.

The key is to act quickly and not put the job search off until later. If you're looking for a retail job, you should start looking a month to two months before the holidays come around, when stores start hiring extra workers for the Christmas rush. Applying early will increase your chances of being the one picked for a job interview.

Putting together a neatly typed resumé (a list of personal information and your school and work experience) can't hurt, either. Although many retail jobs don't require it, having a resumé can help you stand out from the other applicants who don't have one. And a resumé makes it much easier to fill out the application, since you'll have all the information you need in one place.

3. **Where to Look**

There are many places where you can look for a job. The most common are online job boards like Craigslist.org and Monster.com. Lots of individual companies also list available jobs on their websites, and you can often apply online. You should always do this, but unless you really stand out, your chances aren't good.

To improve your chances, you should also actually go out on foot and fill out applications at different places. But before you even set out, you must be dressed appropriately and present yourself in a serious manner. Well-groomed hair, a white shirt, tie, and slacks with dress shoes are the standard. The way you present yourself tells the employer a lot about you. Remember, the first impression should be the best impression.

On a job application you must fill out all the information correctly and neatly, because if you don't they will take your application and say, "We'll call you in a couple of weeks," and then throw it in file 13 (the trash).

If you fill out an application and they don't call you back by the time they say they will, give them a call to let them know that you are really interested in working there. They may actually give you an interview date.

4. **Network to Success**

Another way of finding a job—maybe the best way—is by networking. Networking means talking to people who may know of job openings and letting them know you are interested and available. (Many jobs aren't advertised on job boards, but are passed on by word of mouth.) If you're looking for a job, ask everyone you know—teachers, coaches, friends, friends' parents, neighbors, mentors—if they've heard about any opportunities. And if that person knows you well, and there's an opening at the place they work, he or she can put in a good word for you, which will improve your chances. My director at Youth Communication said he often has jobs that need doing—everything from cleaning to mailings to data entry—that he would not advertise. But if he knew a reliable teen who wanted the job, he'd hire him right away.

> **Another way of finding a job—maybe the best way—is by networking.**

The way I got my job was by going out on foot, filling out applications and handing in resumés in as many places as I could find. I mainly went to department stores, electronic stores, and a lot of other large stores that I knew. (Larger stores tend to hire more, and you won't feel embarrassed asking if they're hiring because there are many other people besides yourself in the office filling out applications.)

A lot places I went to said, "No, we're not hiring," but some said, "Come back in a couple of weeks." Hearing the no's made me feel rejected, but I couldn't give up because if I did, I would be back to Square One (five lint balls and a rubberband).

After a day of job hunting I would go home and anticipate a call from an employer for a job interview. Most of them didn't call, like I predicted, but I got one call to come in for an interview at Macy's.

5. **An Interview**

When I got there I was happy to see that my interviewer was the same person who had taken my application and resumé. First I had to fill out another application, then answer questions on a computer, and finally have a person-to-person interview. The first two were easy, but when I had to go for the interview I was nervous as hell.

> **You have to look for the job, the job isn't going to look for you.**

They called me in. The employer recognized me from the previous time and the interview began. He asked me the big question, "Tell me, why do you want to work at Macy's?"

I said, "Because I would like the experience of a real work environment, and the jobs that I have been on before weren't the type that made me feel like I was part of a real workforce. Macy's is the place where I feel that I can flex my sales abilities."

He asked me how much I would prefer to make an hour. I told him, "Between $7 to $9 an hour." A statement like this gives you a better chance for a higher wage than you expected. You won't limit yourself to just one number, and it's a reasonable amount of money. It will also give the employer some numbers to play with.

(Another important tip is to make your answers to the questions sound intelligent and well thought out. One-word answers and slang are not the way to go.)

After the second question, the employer took another look at

my resumé, nodded his head in approval, stuck out his hand, and said, "Welcome aboard."

At this moment the joy I felt was immeasurable. I was surprised that he had only asked me two questions (most interviews have many more questions), but as I said before, your resumé can speak for you and save you from being asked 99 questions.

6. Last Advice

Many young people look for jobs but give up because they feel that they've looked everywhere. Many teenagers ask me how they can get a job at Macy's. I always tell them to have a resumé because it will make you stand out from the others who don't have one and also to be well-dressed and well-spoken.

Looking for and getting a job is one of the most tedious experiences life has to offer. But if you keep at it, have a positive attitude, and present yourself well, an opportunity will come your way. There's just one important thing to remember—you have to look for the job, the job isn't going to look for you.

Sharif was 19 when he wrote this story. He went on to attend college and work in the computer field.

Going Back to Preschool

By Gamal Jones

1. After story time, the teacher at the preschool where I work chooses fun and different ways to have the children go one at a time to clean up. One morning, she selected the children according to the color of their clothes.

"Anyone wearing brown, please go wash your hands," she said.

Charlie scurried away to the bathroom. Then, in the breathless way that many of the 3- and 4-year-olds in my class often speak, James blurted out, "Gamal—he's, he's, he's wearing brown on his face."

Silence. It lasted for about half of a second. After glancing at me, the teacher, seeming stunned, said something like, "Yes, we all have different-colored skin." I just cracked a slight smile. But boy, oh boy, later on that day I almost split in half laughing every time that moment came to mind.

That's a taste of the creative genius I've been hearing on a regular basis from my young students since last November, when I started working as a teacher's aide at a preschool in West Orange, New Jersey.

2. Encouraging the Little Runts

I first thought of working with children three years ago. My interest stemmed from a combination of wanting more meaningful work than retail, wanting to work close to home, and seeing all the cute female employees at a daycare center across the street from my house.

I figured I could encourage the little runts to be themselves, and they'd inadvertently encourage me to do the same. As I see it, children are the last people left on earth who do and say what they truly feel. But when I applied to the daycare center near my house, I didn't get the job because I lacked experience.

Over the next three years, I had jobs at an auto parts store and a gift shop at the mall. I also got unemployment for five months when I lost my gift shop job. That's when I started volunteering as an artist and a writer for Youth Communication. I liked unleashing my creative side, but the pangs of not working were starting to get to me. I needed something more to do during the week. I also needed money once my unemployment ran out.

3. A Personal Connection and Networking Got Me the Job

During the summer, one of my brothers began to date a lovely young lady, Crystal, who worked as a teacher at a preschool. One day when he picked her up from work, they offered him a job. He already had a good job but he told me about the offer since he thought I'd be interested.

I called Crystal and a few weeks later the educational director scheduled me for an in-person interview. During the interview, she asked me about working at Youth Communication. After some conversation, she told me she knew the executive director at Youth Communication because their daughters go to the same school. Well, what a co-inky dink. I had been networking and I didn't even know it! I was thinking that getting this job might be fate.

Apparently she liked me because she asked me to come in to observe a class and get a feel for the job. I visited the following Tuesday. That day, the children gave me a sneak preview of what to expect. I caught two of them tongue-kissing each other right in front of me. I don't know if they knew what they were doing, but I parted the young ones gently and told them that wasn't the right thing to do.

> **These kids remind me how to interact in a real and honest way.**

The following Monday, I called the preschool to see if I could volunteer again. I wasn't prepared for the educational director to tell me that a part-time position was available, but I was happy about it! I accepted, which made her happy too. She told me I'd work in the mornings and the pay she offered was more than I'd made at my previous jobs.

4. Learning the Routine

I've been working at the preschool for five months now, and I've got the routine down. In the morning, the children play in open areas. Then there's circle time, when the class sings songs. Then the teacher assigns jobs for each kid, like table cleaner, pet feeder, or classroom detective. After that, the teacher picks games for the kids to play.

After they clean up, the teacher reads a story, and the kids wash their hands for snack time. After gobbling up their snacks, they either play outside or in the classroom, depending on the weather. Afterward, they wash up again for lunch. Then it's nap time.

As a teacher's aide, I'm there to handle the odds and ends, snack time and clean up, so the teachers can focus on the students. I also help with the students—maintaining order, making sure they do things the right way, and keeping them safe.

The students are 3- and 4-year-old, middle-class children of pretty diverse backgrounds. Each day, the number of children in the class varies, though the most we'll have in a day is about 17. The majority of the school is white, but three children in my class are of mixed backgrounds and there are some black kids.

I'm learning so much from the two teachers I work with. I love seeing the way they say something only once and the children do exactly what they say, even the rambunctious ones. It's obvious that the teachers' power has grown over time and they have a lot of influence over the children. With me it happens sometimes, but I don't have the glow—that gift of influence over the children—yet.

5. Learning From the Kids

But I already know I love these kids, man. They're hilarious without meaning to be. One day I was sitting next to Audrey, one of the little ladies in the class. She wanted to sing to me.

She stretched her neck out to get the notes just right as she sang some song from the movie *Pocahontas II*. I could barely understand the words, but her enthusiasm, high-pitched and off-key voice, and serious face were priceless comedic gems. I tried to conceal my laughter but I failed miserably.

> **I don't know if teaching small children is what I want to do with my life, but I'd like to stick around for several years.**

I'm learning so much more about human nature than anything I could read in books. I've figured out that people don't really grow up. I swear I've met some of these children before in adult form. The way they interact with one another, the manner in which they deal with problems, success, and their emotions, I've seen in myself and in folks my age and older.

Adults don't behave the exact same way, not by crying and kicking down another student's rocket ship made out of building blocks. But the emotions are the same—we just disguise them better. When we get jealous, hurt, or can't get our way, we write songs, drink, cheat on our partners, or steal.

6. **Improving My Social Skills**

I love and admire how honest children are. And it's not an obnoxious, brutal honesty intended to hurt feelings. It's just honesty. They say what's on their minds, whether they want you to play with them, feed them, or want to tell you that you hurt their feelings. They have their friends in the class they'd rather sit next to, but you could seat any of them next to each other and, for the most part, they could get along and have a conversation.

Decades later, folks like me are afraid to tell our friends we don't like what they're doing with their lives for fear of them getting upset. And men older than me won't ask women out on dates because of their fragmented social skills. But these kids remind me how to interact in a real and honest way.

I don't know if teaching small children is what I want to do with my life, but I'd like to stick around for several years. I heard that the boss ladies work with school schedules, so if I decide to go to college, there shouldn't be any conflict.

And I'd like to get the glow, man. If I could get the best out of these kids, and get them to listen to me without causing any psychological harm, I think I'd be able to understand and deal with almost anybody.

Gamal was 20 when he wrote this story. He continues to work in child care, and also works as an editorial illustrator.

Young and Hungry

By Joseph Alvarez

1. "Wanted: Enthusiastic person for an assistant editor intern position at HBO Studio Production. All inquires please contact Kremer Hoke."

"Man, this sounds like a sweet gig," I thought. I was three years into college, studying video editing. This job fit me like a glove. I stuck the ad in my pocket. I didn't want anybody else to see that!

I headed straight back to my dorm to call Kremer. I was a little nervous but finally worked up my courage to call him.

Ring! Ring!

"HBO Studio Production, how may I help you?"

"Yes, can I speak to Mr. Hoke, please?"

"Speaking."

"Hi, my name is Joseph Alvarez and I'm calling about the assistant editor intern position."

He asked me a few questions and then set me up for an interview. Man, I was happy. I hung up my phone and starting singing and dancing around my dorm. I remember thinking, "This job search stuff is easy!"

2. **Riding the Clouds When I Got My First Internship**

The next day I went to HBO. I had my best gear on. Walking into the building I felt big time. In the waiting area I was thinking, "Damn, everything here looks so clean and expensive." Then I heard a strong voice say, "Hello, Mr. Alvarez, step into my office."

> **Even after I got the job, I never let up. I took on every day as if it were my last day there.**

Kremer interviewed me for about 15 minutes or so and I think I knocked his socks off, because he called his boss into the office and said a bunch of nice things about me, like, "You're looking at the future of HBO."

He took me on as the new intern. Boy was I happy. It felt like I flew home. I was riding the clouds! I was the new HBO Studio Production Assistant Editor Intern Extraordinaire!

3. **I Was Rich!**

When I started the internship, everything was new and a little bit scary, but I was sure I could learn the way things operated. I was young, hungry, and willing to work my butt off. I think they knew that, because they did work my butt off.

As the months went by, I became known around the place as "hard working Joe." I stayed after hours practicing editing until 4 a.m. Some nights I'd venture off and explore HBO's other floors.

The fanciest room was the music studio. I used to creep in there and touch the cool looking buttons. I never could figure out how to play even a CD in that room, but man, I just liked being around all that expensive equipment. I was a high-tech wannabe geek!

My internship lasted six months. As it came to an end, I

thought, "I can't let this slip away." Luckily, they wanted to hire me, at a whopping 15 bucks an hour. I was rich! Hollywood, here I come!

Even after I got the job, I never let up. I took on every day as if it were my last day there. I wanted to prove myself and show everybody who doubted me that I could make it in the real world.

4. **'We Have to Let You Go'**

But just as I started getting comfortable at HBO, the economy went downhill. A lot of companies began making cutbacks, and HBO was no exception. One afternoon the big boss came into the room.

"Joe, can I speak to you?" he said.

"Sure, what's up?"

"Well, Joe, we're going to make cutbacks."

"What do you mean?" I said

"Well, we're going to have to let you go and only use you on a call-to-call basis."

Man, was I crushed. I was in my last year in college. I had my thesis to complete. I had to find a place to live. And now I had to find a new job. What was I going to do?

I thought to myself, "Hey, I can get a new job, no problem. I have HBO under my belt. I'm big time now." But like HBO, other media companies were not hiring either. I spent hours every day faxing and emailing resumes and heard nothing back.

5. **I Lost Hope**

A year went by. I must have sent hundreds of resumes out. Finally I started thinking, "Maybe this is not the right thing for me." But what was I going to do? Film editing was the only thing I had some sort of skill in.

To pay bills, I took miscellaneous jobs, but man did I feel low. I thought, "How can I have a college degree and only be making $7 an hour?" I felt cheated, like everything high school teachers and counselors had been telling me about the value of a degree was a lie.

Real Men

After two years of working odd jobs, the girl I was with left me because I wasn't getting the big money fast enough for her liking. By then, I wasn't even looking for editing jobs anymore. I had lost my drive. The only thing I was thinking about was surviving. I was rundown-looking, couch surfing at my sister's and friends' apartments, barely making it. I was riding a wave of screwed-up luck. I had lost hope.

So many times I'd think, "How could I have gone from college graduate with all the hope in the world, to asking people to stay on their couch?" Man, was I confused. Then I finally got a stroke of good luck.

6. **Getting Help—and Maybe a Break**

One day I went to a youth organization to get help with my resume. The guy handed me a copy of *Represent*, a youth magazine. When I read the magazine, I saw an ad saying that writers could sign up. Even though I had no real writing experience, I called *Represent* the next day. The editor said, "Sure, come on in."

> **I told her I was a film editor. She said, "Oh, my husband is a producer. Maybe he can help you."**

I thought to myself, "It's that easy?" After years of rejections, I couldn't believe it.

When I met the editor, I told her I was a film editor. I don't even think I believed it when I said it, but hey, I needed to say something. What I really was was a broke-down, beat-up 25-year-old kid trying to make it. She said, "Oh, my husband is a producer. Maybe he can help you out."

"She has to be kidding me," I thought. But her husband met with me the next week. He worked for a TV channel for kids and teens called Noggin, and he introduced me to the person in charge of human resources there, who set me up with an interview. I couldn't believe it! The interview went well, but after a few weeks I heard nothing from them.

7. **Networking Leads to My Big Break**

After that, I met with a friend of his at MTV, but that also seemed to lead to nothing. A few months went by and still nothing. At this point, I think I hit rock bottom—or worse. I had gotten my hopes up so high that when nothing came through, I hit the rock and crashed through it. Man, I was under the rock!

I knew I should keep calling Noggin, but by then I had really given up on myself. I wanted nothing to do with false hope.

Then out of the blue the lady I had interviewed with at Noggin called me. She asked, "Are you still interested in the position?" I felt like saying, "Hell yeah!" But I played it cool and politely said, "Sure, I'm still interested."

> **If I hadn't been working constantly on my computer skills and art skills, I would not have been ready for the job.**

She explained to me that it was a freelance job, which basically means they call you when they need you. For the summer they needed me to work on a project that might take seven days a week. I was willing to work all day every day. This was what I had been waiting for.

8. **Re-learning the Job**

The first week was hard. It had been a lonnnnnng time since I'd worked as an editor, and the computer programs are not simple. I was expected to know what I was doing, and I didn't. That first week, everyone was pretty doubtful. I was messing up a lot of basic stuff.

Privately, I was a mess, but I told myself, "You just have to get aggressive." I started staying later to re-learn the programs. I practiced and practiced, because I did not want to lose this job. By week two, all the skills I'd learned years before came back to me in a hurry.

The rest of the summer I was working 10 hour days, five days a week, making $30 an hour. Still, I knew the project would come to an end. I was so worried that I'd be out of a job again, so I did everything I could to present myself as eager and positive. I hoped someone would recognize my hunger and want to keep me around.

When the project was done, they decided to keep me for about 10 days out of the month. Even though the pay is good (almost five times what I was making at odd jobs) I know I need to find some more freelance work. So, as usual, I try to show my bosses how serious and committed I am.

9. Luck and Determination

Right now, I feel I'm pretty much out of the rut, but some days I wonder if my luck could change at any moment and I will find myself almost homeless again. It was only about six months ago that I was begging for work. Who's to say I will have a job a month from now?

But I know that even though it took a lucky break for me to find Noggin, what's really gotten me where I am is my determination and hard work. If I hadn't been working constantly on my computer skills and art skills, I would not have been ready for the job when the luck hit. As they say, when preparation and opportunity meet, you get lucky!

I think I will be just fine, as long as my hunger never goes away.

Joseph was 25 when he wrote this story.

Maxed Out

By Xavier Reyes

1.   **M**y debt problems started when I went to college and got my first credit card. I was 17 years old. Like other college freshman, I was bombarded with credit card applications in the mail.

So I applied, not for one credit card, but for three. As luck would have it, I got approved for all three credit cards.

As soon as my credit cards arrived in the mail, I headed off to shop. At that time I was going through an Adidas phase. With my credit card, I bought a whole lot of Adidas stuff as well as CDs, a radio, and video games. It was amazing. I didn't have to have the money to buy these things, but whatever I wanted was mine.

2.   **How Can I Pay Them?**

When the bills came in, I paid the minimum amount due,

which wasn't more than $25 per card. I thought that as long as I paid the minimum amount each month I would be fine. I didn't know then how credit cards worked. Credit cards charge interest—they take a percentage of the money you owe and add that to the next month's bill.

For instance, say you owe $400. Even if you pay the minimum amount due and don't use the credit card to buy anything else, the next month you will owe more than $400. Believe it or not, it might not be long before the $400 turns into $800.

My bills skyrocketed. Soon I owed $1,800.

At first I wanted to be responsible, so I paid what I could afford. After a while, though, I started to feel like I was trying to climb out of a deep hole, but the more I tried, the more slippery it became. I began to miss payments. Then late fees were added to my bills, which cost a lot—another $30 a month or more!

> **I thought that as long as I paid the minimum amount each month I would be fine.**

Plus, because I had allowed the late charges and penalties to pile up, I was way over my credit limit. So I was also now paying an over-the-limit-fee of $25 each month.

3. **I Got Discouraged**

I reached a point where I thought there was no way I could pay my credit cards back. So I went from making late payments to making no payments at all. I hoped that somehow they would all just disappear.

But they never did.

I got letter after letter telling me that if I did not pay them back it would affect my credit rating. This meant they would write up a report saying I was not good at paying back loans.

I grew concerned. When I graduated from college, I wanted to have my own apartment. I knew that in order to have this, I had to have good credit. No landlord wants a tenant who doesn't repay his debts. The only way I was going to be able to repair my credit was to pay the bills that I had ignored for so long.

By then, I owed $2,100. I began paying as much as I could—which was about $50 per card—but no matter how much I paid, it didn't make a dent in my debt.

Finally I heard about a debt management agency, which would work with my creditors to give me lower interest rates for the amounts I owed. This would make it easier to keep up with my debt, and would also help stop the annoying letters and phone calls that I was getting about my bills, as long as I paid the lower rates reliably. This would last for a couple of years, or until I paid off all the bills.

> **Now I truly resent credit cards. I see them as a trap.**

4. **Trying to Break Free**

Five years later, I am still paying off the credit cards. Right now I owe about $1,000 in credit cards. I have cut up all my cards except for one, which I keep just in case I have an emergency.

It's a burden to have to pay back my debt, especially since I now live on my own. After I get done paying the rent, utilities, phone bill, cable, food, transportation, credit cards and other bills, I barely have $50 left to myself.

Now I truly resent credit cards. I see them as a trap, laced with everything your heart desires (or that your credit limit allows). And to think, I don't even wear Adidas anymore.

Xavier was 22 when he wrote this story. He graduated from college and worked at a major media company.

Chapter 7

Finding Connection

Building Trust, Brick by Brick

By Manny S.

1.   By the time I got sent to my third foster home, when I was 8 years old, I'd started to believe that all my experiences in foster care would be negative. I was trapped in a circle of revolving doors, and I didn't think I'd ever be able to stay in one place.

At my first foster home, there was a kid named Robert who thought he could bully my younger brother Daniel. One day I got so fed up with him that I punched him in the face, and my brother and I got kicked out. Then we were sent to live with my uncle, which was great, until he kicked us out. He said it was because Daniel and I were always fighting.

After getting the boot from my own family, I started to think I couldn't rely on them as much. I figured I could only be independent. I also believed that since I wasn't in those two homes for very long, my next home would be the same.

On my way to my next foster home I thought I'd better be

ready to leave in three or four months, and I was already worried about where I'd get sent next. I was also scared of what my new foster mom would be like. I pictured her as a witch with razor-sharp teeth and claws.

2. No Point in Unpacking

I walked to the door with Daniel and my social worker and rang the bell. I heard barking and I was terrified at what she might have in that house—perhaps a pit bull trained to scare little kids, or torture them as they slept.

The door opened and I saw a woman with a happy face, anxious but full of excitement. She welcomed us in, but I was cautious due to what I'd heard at the door. Then I looked down, and saw a little dog whose bark was way bigger than his bite. I looked around the apartment and I liked what I saw, but I was still on my toes.

The woman said her name was Melba. She showed us our room and told us to make ourselves at home, but I didn't unpack my things just yet. I felt like there was no point since we would be leaving soon anyway. My brother and I stood in the hall as Melba and my social worker talked in the living room. I started to imagine the horrible things she would do or make us do when my social worker left.

When my social worker came in to say goodbye I thought, "Yup, this is it." I heard the door slam shut and my heart started to pound as I heard footsteps closing in toward the room, but I played it cool and sat on the bed. Her mouth opened and just when I thought she was going to breathe fire, she asked, "Are you guys hungry?"

3. Giving Me Space

Daniel said yes, but I said no. I was, but I wasn't comfortable asking her for anything. When she went to use the bathroom, I ran to the kitchen and grabbed a little something to eat.

The first few months were all the same. I would get home from school, go to my room, close the door, and do my homework. When Melba would come by and ask if I was hungry I'd usually say no. She didn't annoy me or force me to eat. She gave me my space, which was what I wanted. At dinnertime, I would just stay in my room.

Most of the time when I was in my bedroom, Melba would come in and ask if I'd finished doing my homework. I have to admit, it felt good to know she cared. We'd sometimes have little awkward encounters when we ran into each other in the house. We'd say "hey" or "hi," but nothing more than that.

> **Melba didn't annoy me or force me to eat. She gave me my space, which was what I wanted.**

After five or six months, I started thinking I might be here longer than I'd thought. I also noticed Melba's consistency when it came to feeding me and checking my homework. Sometimes I'd take some change off her dresser to see how she'd react, but she never seemed frustrated.

4. **Feeling Warmer Inside**

I started to feel a little warmer inside. I began to answer, "Yes," when she asked if I was hungry, and I started leaving the door to my bedroom open. We even started to have conversations about things we liked or had in common. I found out that she'd had other foster children living there, but they were given back to their families. I thought that maybe the same thing would happen to me.

I felt happy that under Melba's care those kids had "survived" long enough to be returned to their families. I felt she could do the same for me until I was reunited with my family. This let me feel comfortable trusting Melba. Pretty soon I started to hug her when I came home from school, and I started showing her more affection than any of my previous foster moms.

On my 9th birthday, Melba took Daniel and me to the World

Trade Center, which I'd never visited (this was before 9/11). When we got to a huge building that towered over me, she said, "We're here." I thought that we were going to do something boring, but I was shocked when we got inside. There was actually a huge variety of stores and restaurants. I'd never seen anything like it in my entire life.

5. Part of the Family

We looked at everything and we got to eat pizza at a cool restaurant, which I wasn't used to. When we sat down I tried to think of the last time I'd eaten at a table like that. I was so happy that she remembered my birthday, took me somewhere, and had gotten me a present.

After that, I opened up a lot more. I believed that Melba had paid her dues and earned her stripes as my foster mom. I started talking to Melba a lot, and I often found myself the one starting the conversations. We'd talk about the news, school, TV, and anything else worth talking about. The conversations weren't three hours long, but they were progress nonetheless. I also began to get closer to her family, which was cool. They didn't live with us, but they all treated me as if I was really part of their family.

> **I started to feel a little warmer inside, and started leaving the door to my room open.**

Around the time I turned 14, I realized adoption was a possibility. We didn't really talk about it, but as time went on I knew that eventually it had to happen.

6. 'I'm Here for You'

One day Melba sat me on the couch and said, "If you want to be adopted, I am here for you." I had grown to love Melba, but the idea that I couldn't live with my parents again seemed weird to me, and made me sad. I had to think about my situation before I could make a decision.

For years, my birth mother had filled my head with the dream that I'd be going home. But it never happened. Every time she made a promise that I could go home and then didn't keep it, I felt knocked down to the ground. That's when my mother would come again and lift up me up, only to knock me down again. But eventually, I got used to her routine.

7. Making It Permanent

When I finally realized that going back home wasn't going to happen, I knew that adoption was what I wanted. Now we're in the process of making that happen.

Melba has already been my parent for so long; the only thing that the adoption will change is that my brother and I will legally belong to her. Melba has given me advice and taught me those life lessons that you need to succeed, like saving money, helping people, and taking school seriously.

Melba and I have developed a bond over the past several years. I am happy that I finally got a break from the negativity, and soon it will be permanent. Melba has been my salvation from a dramatic and awful life. We started from one brick and built a skyscraper of trust, understanding, and love.

Manny was 15 when he wrote this story. He was later adopted, and graduated from high school.

Opening Up to My Shorty

By Antwaun Garcia

1. Once in a while someone finally grows up and realizes what he wants. In my case, I went from being what you would call a pimp, a playa, someone who doesn't care about other people's feelings, to someone who is trying hard to settle down and be caring.

   In all of my previous relationships I have cheated on a female with one or numerous other females. I didn't care too much about their feelings. I used females like a boy uses a toy.

   Back in those days I used to have what I called "a phase" with a female. I would gas her head up like I needed her, like she was everything to me. (It was easy for me to tell girls nice things when I didn't mean them.) Then, poof, out of nowhere I'd let her know it was over. I could never face rejection so I would hand it out before it came to me.

2. **'Bye-Bye-Bye'**

    I would toss her number away, toss her letters, toss any pics of us, too. Kind of cold-hearted, I know, but it's the truth. I would have females depressed thinking about me, wondering what I might be doing. My way of getting over a female was to just bag another one. Then, once again, after about a month, it was "bye-bye-bye."

    I knew I didn't want to be like two of my boys, who were almost devastated when their girls left them. I'd hear cats in the streets complaining, "My girl left me." But that wasn't my way.

    But after a while, I started getting annoyed at females who only cared how thick my pockets were. I wanted to settle down, to have a wifey to go places with and to miss when she's not with me.

3. **I Wanted to Stick With Someone**

    Now, believe it or not, I think I have found that one. At the time we started talking, I was talking to five other girls, and she was talking to some cornball around her way. We were both tired of these corny people and wanted something serious. I will admit, I wasn't planning to be faithful to her at first. But she opened my eyes to the fact that she wasn't a dummy I would talk to and get my way with.

    Now I have been dating her for the past 10 months, and to be honest they have been the best 10 months I have ever spent with any girl. She

    > **It was easy for me to tell girls nice things when I didn't mean them.**

    is mad cool and mad funny. She has a great personality and is a very good listener. Normally I don't talk to anyone about the drama in my life, but my shorty has always opened her ear to me.

4. **We Had Great Convos**

    One week, we were talking on the phone from 10 at night till

4 in the morning when we both had to be at school early the next day. It wasn't one of those boring convos like, "The sky is blue and the grass is green." We were really talking, really getting to know one another, really laughing the whole six or seven hours on the phone each day of that week. I had never done that with any female before.

I couldn't get enough of this girl. When we had class together we would sit next to one another and talk through the whole class, or write notes and crack jokes. Afterwards we would get something to eat up the block at the bagel shop, and then I would walk her to the bus. We did that from February to the end of the school year.

> **I wanted to get better at showing my feelings not just for my shorty, but because I wanted to be able to show my feelings to my family, too.**

5. **Opposites Attract**

What's real interesting is we have nothing in common yet we are so compatible. She loves bacon. I hate pork. She loves horror films. I think they are corny and prefer a comedy or action film. She listens to rock and roll, and I listen to r&b and rap. Yet we still find similarities within one another.

And over the last 10 months, she has always been there for me, no matter what. I have been through some tough times, and she stood by me through it all. She listened about my life and past. She couldn't believe how I survived what I've been through. It kind of left her speechless. But telling her about my past helped her understand why I am the person I am. She loves me for who I am.

The main problem I have with her and most females I've liked is letting my feelings show. Don't get me wrong, I've told females what they want to hear, but usually when I don't mean it. It's hard for me to tell my feelings when they're real. After all,

I have kept my feelings bottled up since I was 10, the year two of my best friends died. They were the only two people I confided my feelings in. When I lost them, I felt like I couldn't talk to anyone else, and not talking about my feelings became a habit.

6. Could I Say How I Felt?

But with my shorty, I wanted to tell her my feelings. It just seemed like a big risk. What if I told her how I felt and we soon ended things? Then I might feel mad and stupid for showing her my vulnerable side. I might be heartbroken, or feel pitiful and depressed.

But I knew I'd feel just as bad if the relationship ended and I never told her how I felt, or, worse, if it ended *because* I never told her how I felt. I decided that growing in relationships is all about showing people how you feel, and taking a chance by trusting them with your soft side.

Even if there are grimy people in the world, that didn't mean my shorty was one of them. I could work at letting my feelings show, at my own pace, to make our relationship even better. And I wanted to get better at showing my feelings not just for her, but because I wanted to be able to show my feelings to my family, too. For most of my life, my pride and stubbornness and fear that I can't trust people have prevented me from doing that. So even though I was nervous about saying how I felt, I decided I was up for the challenge.

7. Trying to Open Up

I started by trying to tell her all I thought and felt, the good as well as the bad. Then I started trying to express the emotions I would rather not expose, like telling her when I miss her. She responds like any typical female. She says stuff like, "That was so cute."

I'm getting more comfortable telling her what I think and feel, but expressing those emotions I don't feel like talking about isn't getting easier. Sometimes my girlfriend won't realize how hard it is for me, and she will change the subject or even start singing or acting stupid when I'm about to say something I really need to say. That's when I think, "Either I'm boring her or she doesn't want to hear it." Then I stop talking and don't say anything more until she asks me to. It takes a lot of trust to expose my innermost thoughts and feelings.

Now that we are getting deeper into the relationship my feelings are growing. We talk every night. No matter the time, we always make sure we put one another to sleep. But at the same time, I am still taking my time with showing her my feelings, because we both don't want to rush into something we are not ready for.

As I am growing older and more mature, I don't find the same things fun anymore. The idea of playing a female intentionally just doesn't sound fun. What sounds better is trying to build a good relationship by working to trust and be trustworthy, and showing my feelings more. I am respecting females a little more, and I'm feeling the benefits of it.

Antwaun was 18 when he wrote this story.

I Have Faith in My Church

By Stephen Simpson

1. **A**ny Sunday, at noon. Everyone is seated, the musicians are warming up (Deacon Connell on the keys and Eric on the drums). The front line singers are in position, and the worship leader is just about ready to start.

    There is a smile on most faces in the congregation, and some exchange pleasantries. Bright "Our Harvests Are Great In 1998" banners decorate the inside of 4420 Seton Ave. in the Bronx.

    "Let us all stand..." the worship leader starts off. Another service at Overcoming Faith Ministries is about to begin.

2. **Everyone's Having a Good Time**

    I started coming to Overcoming Faith Ministries three years ago, and I've learned a lot from the pastor and from the other members of the congregation. The people at my church are very open, and because it's so small (around 60 or 70 people), it's easy to get to know everybody. When we give praise and worship, it's hard not to get involved. When I see everyone singing, clapping, and having a good time, I try to join in and enjoy myself, too.

I like church the best when the choirs sing. We have three main choirs, so you never know who's getting called until they do. All the choirs sound good, and when you're sitting in that pew, it's nice to hear a sweet sound in your ear.

> **The people at my church are very open, and because it's so small, it's easy to get to know everybody.**

I also like when people stand up to give their testimony. Sometimes their words will encourage others enough to get them through their own situations. People testify about things like healing from illnesses or deliverance from drugs. It's encouraging because you can understand what Jesus has done in their lives.

3. **After Services, the Whole Church Hangs**

You can see how close the congregation is after the services when the whole church hangs! There are times when we let out at 3 o'clock, and the church won't get locked up until after 4. We have two main church services (Friday and Sunday), and when church is through, we will sit down and talk and talk and talk and….you get the picture.

People talk about future plans, work they need to start or finish, and other things you might tell a friend. I usually hang outside with my friends after church, but sometimes I'll go inside and talk to one or two adults.

If it gets too late, the pastor sometimes has to force everyone out of the church. That's what I love about my church, the fellowship that we share with one another.

4. **Good Advice...and Groceries When Needed**

I also talk to my pastor (Barbara Connell), but not very often.

When we do talk, it will be about God or something that happened to me, and she'll give me advice.

I don't think she bases her sermons on the congregation's circumstances on purpose, but 90% of her sermons hit a spot where you are now, have been, or are on your way to. The values she stresses to us are faith in God, prayer, family unity, and love.

Outside of church, Pastor Connell is a constant help to my family and to the other families in the congregation. Since most adults at the church are single parents, she's always being looked to for support.

When my family was going through a rough time, pastor and the church stepped right in and helped us get everything under control again. She provided groceries for us when we needed them, helped us if we needed money, and counseled our family.

At first, I didn't know where the money and supplies were coming from. When I found out that she was behind it, that made me feel good because I had never heard of a church helping out so much before. The Bible says to help one another, but this was the first church that ever helped us like that.

> **I get a sense of community, love, and guidance from my church that I don't get anywhere else.**

5. **Keeping Each Other on Track**

I'm impressed that Pastor Connell tries to make herself such a good example (she is) for everyone to follow. She doesn't tell you to do anything she wouldn't do herself.

I get a sense of community, love, and guidance from my church that I don't get anywhere else. We help keep each other standing. (If it seems like I'm repeating "help," it's because that's what we do.)

I believe Overcoming Faith Ministries is different from many other churches because it's so small. At many churches you find social groups, the gossip corner and the "peanut gallery," but we don't have that.

Again, we're not perfect and we do slip, but here you can feel assured that if you do get off track, you don't have to stay off track, because someone will try to help you to your feet.

Stephen was 17 when he wrote this story. He went on to graduate from high school and go to college.

Some POPS Are Hanging In

By Antwaun Garcia

1.   **O**ne day when I was about 8 or 9, my dad and I were walking down 125th Street in Harlem, New York. A girl walked past and he bet me $5 he could get her phone number. He talked to her and came back with a lipstick kiss on his cheek and a paper with her name and number on it.

"Where's my money?" he asked me.

My father was living with my mother, sister, two brothers and me then, but I knew he wasn't much of a family man. He was always in and out of prison. He would show up and then disappear for two or three years—the same routine over and over. I missed having a dad to help me learn how to read and write, to play sports with and talk to. I wanted him to help me answer questions such as, "Can I make it in life?" and, "What is my purpose?" I've constantly thought to myself, "Why didn't he want any part of me?"

I'm not alone in missing a dad. More than half of all black children don't live with their fathers, according to the U.S. Census Bureau. And at least one in three Hispanic kids and one in four white kids live without their dads. I thought the numbers would be even worse. So many people I know don't have a father.

2. **Striving to Be a Top Pop**

To better understand why so many men are not taking care of their kids, I went to a program called POPS (Providing Opportunity for Parental Success) in Harlem. POPS works mostly with black and Latino fathers who are 18 to 35 years old. The eight-week workshop helps fathers reunite and connect with their children, and POPS also offers counseling, mediation with family members, and legal help.

Robert Sanchez, the program manager, told me that POPs doesn't give up on guys and tells them not to give up on having a good relationship with their kids, even if a dad is told he can't see his kids or feels the kid doesn't appreciate him. Once a man participates in POPs, he can come back for help throughout his entire life. "We're like a leech. We latch on and don't let go," Sanchez said.

> **I'm not alone in missing a dad. More than half of all black children don't live with their fathers.**

Sanchez struck me as cool and relaxed, but I found he could relate in a personal way to breaking the cycle of fatherlessness. He caught me off guard because he was dressed in a suit, but actually, he had a little bit of the hood in him. Sanchez didn't get to know his own father until he was 15 years old. And later, he struggled to stay connected to his own daughter during the 15 years when he was in prison.

3. **Fatherhood and Fear**

Research shows that kids who don't have dads are much more likely to be poor, depressed, fail school, commit crimes, have sex early on and (for girls) get pregnant. Why would a man put his kids at such risk? The main reason, Sanchez said, is fear. Having a child is scary! A lot of guys worry that they don't know how to care for a child and don't want to look stupid.

Some men don't stay because of baby mama drama. "Fifty percent of our fathers have a volatile relationship with their child's mother," and almost none are married to them, he noted. Frustrated with their child's mother, men may stop seeing their kids to avoid conflict. Or, the mothers may not let them visit.

Other dads disappear because they get caught up in the streets or prison. And lots of fathers have no idea how to be a good parent because they never had one themselves. At

> **A father is not just a roll of bills, but "a guiding light, a teacher, a friend, a protector, an enlightener, and a supporter."**

least 15% of the men who participate in POPS were in foster care when they were boys, Sanchez said.

Many men believe a father's only role is to provide for their children. Men with jobs are more likely to be present in their children's lives. Those without money often don't stick around because "they associate fatherhood as an extension of their pocket, and think 'I'll stay out of the child's life until I have money,'" Sanchez explained.

4. Not Just a 'Roll of Bills'

But even the poorest fathers can support their children in important ways, Sanchez said. A father is not just a roll of bills, but "a guiding light, a teacher, a friend, a protector, an enlightener. A father is a supporter, someone you can go to for understanding and love.

"One question I ask the fathers is, 'What is one great thing you remember about your dad?'" Their answers, Sanchez said, never have to do with how much money their fathers spent on them. "That child is not going to remember the sneakers, but he does remember the time you took him to the park, or to a baseball game, or made him feel good about himself."

Real fatherhood, said Sanchez, is "if you gave them a hug every day," spend time with them, and show you really care about their feelings. In POPS, dads learn how to hold a newborn and how a baby communicates his needs by crying. POPs shows men how easy it is to play with their children, help them with homework, ask about their interests, or discover something new by taking kids on outings. Dads learn child development, how to be patient, and how to solve a child's problems without criticizing a child or making her feel bad.

If the mother won't let a dad see his kids, POPS workers take the dad to family court and show him how to establish paternity, get a visitation order, and enforce his legal rights to see his children.

5. **It's Personal**

Sanchez's own history explains why he is so passionate about fatherhood. At 18, Sanchez fathered a daughter. He was also arrested in an apartment where drugs were found and sent to prison for 15 years. While incarcerated, he wrote his daughter, had visits with her, and kept communication open with his daughter's mother.

When he came out of prison, his feelings were hurt because he bought his daughter a cellphone to stay in touch with him and she didn't call him much.

One day Sanchez watched a Spanish flick, "Mi Familia," that showed a character returning from prison and trying to force his child into a relationship. The child rejects him. An older, wiser relative tells the man, "You can't come home and demand a relationship."

"That, to me, was a lesson," said Sanchez.

The movie helped him understand that fathers must be patient and that it takes children a long time to learn to trust someone who left them. His daughter was a little afraid he would make new rules for her and try to control her, Sanchez explained. "Her feelings were legitimate. I had been out of her life for 14 years and had to give her space and room to feel what she's feeling."

Sanchez let his daughter know he would always be there for her, but that she could have some say in how much time they would spend together. Now they see each other about twice a month, when she comes to New York. (She lives in Massachusetts.)

> **In order to be a good father, you need to understand your own anger, your past, and your parents.**

"She's in a rebellious stage and a father is the perfect person to be rebellious against," Sanchez explained.

6. Find a Role Model

When Sanchez was released from prison, he made friends with people he trusted to help him out when he felt stuck or confused. "I made it my business to know what a father was, with positive fathers and role models around me."

He encourages dads at POPS to search for mentors to help them. A good role model is someone who is accountable (shows up when he says he will and keeps his promises), takes responsibility when he makes mistakes (admits he's wrong, apologizes, and makes amends), and knows how to listen without criticizing. Once you find one, "tell him that you admire him and ask if he can give you guidance," Sanchez advised.

7. Breaking the Cycle

In order to be a good father, you need to understand your own anger, your past, and your parents, Sanchez explained. Sanchez wanted to break his own family's cycle of father absence so badly he was willing to do things that were new and uncomfortable for him, like not using drugs or alcohol, forgiving people who wronged him, going back to school (he earned a master's degree in urban theology), and traveling all over the world.

I always believed that it was easy for some fathers to give up on raising their children. Now I know that there are fathers, like Sanchez and those in POPS and other fatherhood programs, who are out there trying to stay in the lives of their children. They want to break the cycle. When it's my turn, I'm going to try to break mine as well.

Antwaun was 21 when he wrote this story.
He later became a manager at a major hardware retailer.

Becoming a Father

By Michael Orr

1.   **G**rowing up, a lot of my friends looked up to me as a father figure. I think they saw me that way because they trusted me and could rely on me whenever they needed me. I was their right-hand man. I am a good listener; I don't run on people in needy situations and that's what my friends liked about me. But I never really pictured myself actually being someone's father until now.

   In November of '06 my girlfriend, Erica, and I found out she was pregnant. I was surprised.

   Erica and I were already living together at the time, in my one-bedroom apartment near the Bronx Zoo. We'd been together for two years and had a pretty good relationship. But we hadn't planned on having kids together. Finding out Erica was pregnant with my baby gave me mixed emotions. I was excited to be able to start a new chapter in my life, but I was worried about how

Erica would be feeling.

She was nervous, and I was too. Since I didn't get the chance to prepare before the pregnancy I decided to get prepared soon after we got home that night. I went online to find information about fatherhood. It was interesting to find out things like the different ways fathers can bond with their babies and how important it is for a father to be a part of his child's life. It made the whole becoming a father thing more realistic to me, and the information set my mind at rest.

2. Trying to Prepare

I accompanied Erica to prenatal classes where we learned what to expect. The most important thing I learned was how to hold a baby. Before, I feared I would hold the baby too tight, but being taught the proper way to hold a baby put my fear at ease. I no longer felt like I would suffocate the baby by holding her the wrong way.

I also asked my father for advice, because he did a fine job raising me and my other siblings. My father has played a really big role in my life. He mostly raised me when I was a child and we always have had a good relationship. Even when we weren't living together we stayed close, and our bond is still going strong.

The kind of advice I was looking for was if he was as scared as I was about having to raise girls, and how he went about it the first year of raising my sisters. My dad communicated with my sisters well and I hope I'll be able to have a healthy communication with my daughter, too.

My father didn't really say much when I asked him about how he handled having both my sisters before he had me and my brother. He just told me that it would take some time getting used to, but after a while things would fall into place. Having the conversation with my father made me feel more confident that I could be a good father to my daughter.

I'd done a lot to get myself the practical information I needed to know how to parent a baby, and I was proud of myself. Not only did I feel prepared, but more confident that I would do whatever it takes to be a dependable father. Now all I had to do was execute everything I had learned.

3. **Connecting the Past and the Future**

July 1, 2007 was when I held my daughter in my arms for the first time. She was 6 pounds and 9 ounces with a head full of hair. I couldn't feel a thing. All the feelings didn't sink in until after I left the hospital because I couldn't stay overnight. I sat in the cab going home, looking out the window and thinking to myself.

I thought about my sister Stephanie, who passed away last year, and how I wished she was there to share the joy

> **I accompanied Erica to prenatal classes where we learned what to expect.**

with me. I knew if she was still alive she would have fallen in love with the baby, and it hurts to think that my daughter will never meet her aunt. When Emma gets a little older I will tell her all about her aunt Stephanie from the time that we were little till the last days before she passed away.

I also thought about memories I had of my dad, about how we bonded, how he always talked to me regardless of whether the situations were good or bad, and showed me how to look out for trouble and how to avoid it. I pictured myself in my dad's place and the baby in my place. I could see myself helping her to grow as much as my dad did with me.

4. **Life as a New Dad**

Since we brought our baby home from the hospital, I've had a lot of important moments with Emma Frost (the nickname I gave her). Moments like her Christening, her first Thanksgiving, and her first Christmas are a grace to me.

I am proud to be able to witness Emma growing up. Not every dad gets to witness the joys I've seen so far, because a lot of dads are not around for their kids. I am making it a priority to be there for my baby as my dad was always there for me. Just watching her grow month to month, seeing her coo, grab her feet and sit up is a joy to me.

Of course, some things have been difficult. For a while it was hard for me to be active with Emma because I wouldn't get enough sleep due to her heavy overnight crying, and I would be dead tired. Now she sleeps through the night, and since I get more sleep it's much easier for me to keep up with her energetic self.

There are days where things are hard, but easier days follow, so whenever I am having a hard time with caring for Emma, I just remain calm and hope that the next day will be much easier.

> **I have become a better person since I've stepped into fatherhood.**

My relationship with Erica is working out well as long as we keep coming together and raising our baby as a team. We're attending couples therapy and whatever problems we have we battle it out in therapy. In the future, I hope we'll get married, but at this point we are just working on getting situated with the baby.

5. **Big Changes**

My relationship with my dad now is going well, too. We get to spend a little more time together than we used to, and I am thankful that he comes to visit the house on some weekends to spend not only father-and-son time with me, but also to spend some time with the baby. He rocks her in such a lovely way and it braces my sprits to see them bonding together. I am glad that he supports me with my decision to build a family.

A lot has happened in my life these past few years. I got my own place, started and maintained a relationship with Erica, met Erica's family, began to see my extended family members again, and dealt with changes with my friends, the loss of my sister, and now the birth of my daughter. All of these changes have helped me to become a more experienced person and a better father for Emma.

The biggest change has been my relationship with myself as a father. I have become a better person since I've stepped into fatherhood. I gained the courage to get out there and find work after being out of work for so long due to an injury. I am slowly reconnecting with family members I became distant with when I went into foster care, because I want my daughter to be around most of her family.

Even though working full-time means I spend less time at home now, my relationship with Emma has strengthened, because for the first time in my life I am doing something positive not only for myself, but for my daughter's well-being. I hope that Emma can look toward me as a good role model as she grows up. Maybe she will find a genuine guy like her father when she gets of age to start dating who will support her in every way, like I am supportive of her mother.

Michael was 21 when he wrote this story. He and Erica later married and had another daughter.

STORIES TO ACCOMPANY
ALTERNATIVE HIGH

The *Real Men* curriculum includes a DVD and a Leader's Guide. The 15-minute DVD, called *Alternative High,* is the true story of how Troy Shawn Welcome, the author of several essays in this book, went from high school dropout to high school principal. Two of the stories that the film was based on, along with a transcript that continues where the film left off, are included in this section.

The Leader's Guide includes lessons to accompany all of the stories in *Real Men*. If you would like information on the DVD or the Leader's Guide, contact lchan@youthcomm.org, or go to www.youthcomm.org.

My School Is Like a Family

By Troy Shawn Welcome

1. I used to go to Harding HS* in the Bronx and I hated it. It was cold and unfeeling—as close to being put in an institution as I ever want to get. The teachers only cared about the work; it seemed they could care less about any problems a student might be dealing with.

The students weren't much better. They were there to show off and try to be cool. I was dealing with a lot of personal problems at the time, and going to a big, impersonal teaching facility with metal detectors and I.D. scanners wasn't helping me at all.

I started getting more and more depressed and began to cut classes. At one point, I stopped going to school altogether.

Meanwhile, my guidance counselor was trying to talk me into applying to a small alternative high school called University

---

Name changed to protect the guilty.

Heights. She said it was a school that would allow me to work at my own pace and I wouldn't be as stressed as I was at Harding. She kept talking about how the teachers and students were on a first name basis, and that they had a class called "Family Group," where people would talk to each other about their problems.

It all sounded good but I didn't feel like adjusting to a new school, new people, and a whole load of new work.

2. Taking the Plunge

She tried to get me to apply there for about a year, but I wasn't budging. Then, in the 11th grade, I heard that my best friend, Eric, had applied and was accepted. He would tell me about how free the atmosphere was and how good some of the girls looked. I asked him to pick up an application for me and, with my counselor's help, I filled it out.

It took a couple of visits and a lot of hard work to get me in. I had to spend a day there and basically be interrogated by the other students, who play an important part in deciding who is and who isn't right for the school. After that they still didn't want to let me in because I had too many credits to transfer, but my counselor kept calling and pleading with them and, in the end, I was accepted.

It was a relief to know that I was finally going to get away from Harding and be able to start a new life. I wanted to leave all my personal and scholastic problems behind. Leaving Harding symbolized the beginning of a new era for me.

All the new students had to go to an orientation during the summer where we played a bunch of "icebreaker" games. So by the first day of school we already knew each other. And University Heights has fewer than 400 students (Harding has about 3,500), so everyone gets to know each other quickly anyway.

My first month at University Heights wasn't what I'd expected. When I heard the word "alternative," I thought that there would be a lot of people who were put there because they had a record of fighting, or who had been expelled from other schools. It wasn't like that.

I felt at home there almost right away. I was finally getting what I didn't have at Harding—a feeling that I belonged. At University Heights there wasn't that much fronting going on. I found myself talking to other students about my personal life and taking their advice.

3. **Mutual Support**

Once we were in class and I was talking about my problems with my father when I suddenly got very emotional. I got up and left the room so the others wouldn't see me cry. Qwana, another student who didn't even know me that well, came out into the hall after me and held me. I never experienced anything like that at Harding—I don't think anyone did. I didn't even know it was possible.

> **There wasn't that much fronting going on. I found myself talking to other students about my personal life.**

I didn't know there were other ways of teaching, either. For one thing, the classes are not overcrowded. And the teachers don't just write on the blackboard and have you copy the notes.

In Spanish class, for example, the learning is interactive. Frank, one of my Spanish teachers, would write the verbs that we were learning that week on the blackboard and then break the class up into groups of four or five. Each group would have to work together to make sentences with the verbs and the adjectives that we had studied the week before. Then we'd have a contest to see which group made the best sentences. It made you forget you were in class and helped you get to know your peers better.

4. **Teachers Who Care**

The teachers at University Heights are good people. They

have the rare ability to care about their students' lives while still doing their job. Michelle teaches Family Group, which is kind of like homeroom. She understands that students sometimes have problems and she tries to help as much as she can, but she also knows how to get under your skin until you do things right.

My friend Sean would miss some days of school and Michelle would nag him to make up his work. After he spoke to her and she understood that he had financial problems, she helped him get a job in the school. That way she was able to keep an eye on him and he could make some money. Sometimes she gets on our nerves with the nagging, but the people who love you will always annoy you once in a while.

> **I've changed... I'm a more intelligent, secure, and decisive man who knows that my only limits are in my imagination.**

Gus, who teaches gym, is another teacher who's really cool. He always seemed like he was a friend more than a teacher. He would go out of his way to help me with my work and he used to lift weights and play basketball and volleyball with us. Every time I see him now, he's always calling me the future writer. He's always saying that he's going to see me on television reporting the news some day. Gus makes me feel good to be who I am.

5. **Students Who Count**

I always feel respected and cared for by my teachers at University Heights. If I don't, I'll tell them and we'll resolve it. I remember when Marion, one of my teachers, interrupted me when I was talking one time in class. I didn't say anything to her but she could tell that I was upset. She approached me in the hallway and said that she didn't mean to cut me off, but time was running out. I accepted her apology. To tell you the truth, I was shocked that she took the time to apologize to a student.

Now that I'm about to graduate from University Heights, I

realize that many things about it have helped to make me a better person. Number one is that I always feel like I'm important there. The teachers care about me and not just the work I do. Knowing that has made a big difference in the amount of effort I put into my work and in my feelings about myself and my future.

I left Harding an extremely insecure, scared, confused teenager who wasn't sure what I'd be doing with my life. But, with the presence of caring teachers and friends and as many memories as a person could hope to get in a single year, I've changed. I'm leaving University Heights an ambitious, more intelligent, secure, and decisive man who knows that my only limits are in my imagination.

Troy's experience at University Heights is dramatized in the DVD Alternative High.

My First Semester: Overworked, Underpaid, and Unprepared

By Troy Shawn Welcome

1.   When I was younger, I used to imagine what my life after high school would be like. I saw myself going away to college and living in a dormitory, meeting new people and having new experiences. I never thought that I would have any difficulty merging onto the highway of adult life. Now, almost a year has passed since I graduated from high school and I've found that making it in the world of responsibilities, bills, priorities, and decisions is harder than I thought.

When the time came to apply to college, I was sure of only one thing—that I wanted to go away. I never wanted to attend school in the city because there are too many distractions here. I worried that I would be hanging out with my friends too much and not devoting enough time to studying. So I decided to apply to a few state schools and to Sarah Lawrence College, a private school about 30 minutes from the city in Bronxville, New York.

As a last resort I also applied to some city colleges.

I found out about Sarah Lawrence from the guidance counselor at my high school. He went to college there and told me that the school was famous for its writing program. Since I was what some people considered a born writer, he thought Sarah Lawrence would be perfect for me.

2. **My Dream School**

After I visited Sarah Lawrence's campus for a weekend I thought it was perfect for me also. Most of the people were friendly and found time in their schedules to entertain me. I went to a party on campus, played pool with some other students, and saw a movie in the campus theater. I liked the atmosphere.

While I was there, I also attended a couple of classes so I could get an idea of what the work was like. I went to a literature class on Saturday morning and most of the people there looked as if they had slept in the classroom, including the professor. It shows a lot when people are comfortable enough to go to class in what looks like their pajamas. I've always felt that small, comfortable classes served better than large, impersonal ones. I left that Sunday with a love for Sarah Lawrence and the idea that I could spend the next four years there.

3. **Scrambling for a Second Choice**

Unfortunately, I wasn't accepted, and that's when my problems started. I wasn't particularly interested in going to any of the state schools—I hadn't even completed the applications. I had thought I was a shoo-in for Sarah Lawrence. I had only considered public schools in the first place because my counselor had told me that it's better to apply to a lot of schools so that I'd have some choices. I guess he was right.

Since I had completed my CUNY (City University of New York) applications, I still had the option of going to a city school. I had heard many good things about one of the schools, Baruch, from my counselor, so it became my first choice. Luckily, Baruch also chose me.

At first, I was excited to know that I'd be going to Baruch. Actually, I was excited to be going anywhere. It was extremely important to me to get a college education because I'd be only the second person in my family to attend college. (My brother was the first.) In all the excitement I can't say that I really envisioned what the first day would be like, but I sure didn't expect what I saw at registration.

4. The First Day Was Hell

When I walked into the registration building at Baruch I experienced what I consider "college hell." There were people on lines, on stairs, in front and in back of me. They all looked confused and upset. I wondered what the problem was.

I had a 3 o'clock appointment, so I strolled over to the right line, secure in the knowledge that I already had my schedule planned out. I had attended a summer orientation where I was given the fall semester course catalogue and instructed on how to arrange my schedule.

I soon found out that none of that mattered. The guy circling the room wasn't handing out college leaflets; he was handing out lists of available courses. Every 15 minutes, he came around with a new list—it seemed that the longer I stood on line, the more courses got closed. Wait a minute! All the classes I was planning to take had been filled. What was I supposed to do now?

My mind was scrambling for answers when I began to notice the two other packed lines that were ahead of the one I was on. Those people had appointments for 1:45 and 2:30. The majority of them were squatted on the floor—they had been waiting so long that their legs wore out. It was then that I got the courage to glance at my watch. It was already 4:30 and I was frustrated (my appointment was for 3 p.m., remember?). And I had to be at work by 6.

5. I Needed a Paycheck

I changed my schedule two more times while on line and then

three more as I sat with the counselor. Then I walked towards the cashier to pay for the scraps I ended up with. I was given African Studies, psychology and the usual math and English courses.

By the time I was three weeks into the semester, I was already having to force myself to go to class. My African Studies course was one of the straws that broke the camel's back. It was a lecture class, which should've been easy. We just had to read certain chapters in our textbook along with attending lectures.

Since I hardly had time to work full-time and read books, I tried to get as much as I could from the lectures. But the professor had a very thick accent and I needed an interpreter to understand 90% of what was being said. That's when I started falling behind.

My psychology class was better. Even though there were about 500 students, the two professors who taught it always added a dash of humor to their lectures, which made it fun. But the fact that it was the only class I had on Tuesday afternoons was a problem.

> **By the time I was three weeks into the semester, I was already having to force myself to go to class.**

I was working nights (from 6 p.m. to 12:30 a.m.) and after sleeping most of the day, I hated having to go downtown for a 3 o'clock class and then rush back uptown to get to work on time. I was putting more value on my paycheck than my education. I used to say that if school would pay me I would go more often.

6. **It Didn't Feel Like College**

The biggest problem was that I didn't feel like I was experiencing college life. Baruch didn't have dormitories, a large campus, or the feel of college. Most of the people there, myself included, just went in, went to class, and then went to work. But that wasn't what I wanted.

I had wanted to live on a campus away from my usual environment. I had wanted school to be my life for four years.

I wanted to eat, sleep, and party in or around my campus. I wanted to feel connected to the other students. But most of the people who attend CUNY schools are too busy trying to support themselves while educating themselves to have time to experience each other.

Since I wasn't getting what I wanted out of college, I quickly grew tired of working long and hard just to pay for books and that ridiculous tuition. To make a long story short, I ended up leaving school in the middle of my first semester, after only three months.

> **Failing was my way of rebelling.**

It wasn't until I left school that I realized why I'd failed at one of the most crucial challenges of my life. I think I set myself up to fail because I never dreamed of going to school in the city. I had always imagined myself on a college campus away from everyone and everything I had grown accustomed to during the last 19 years of my life. So when I had to attend a city school, failing was my way of rebelling.

7. **Wasting My Life Away**

I came to the conclusion that I wasn't ready for college, or maybe I was too lazy. After I left school, I continued working as a telephone interviewer with full-time hours. It wasn't a difficult job. All I had to do for eight hours a night was call people across the nation and type their answers to surveys into a computer. But I felt like my life was worthless.

When I was in school I felt a little productive, but now all I did was work all night and sleep all day. I felt like I was wasting my pitiful life away. My job wasn't even stable—there wasn't always a lot of work, so I couldn't even rely on my checks being the same amount every payday.

I finally quit, thinking I could find a better job and start to make a decent living for myself until I was ready to go back to school. Truthfully, I didn't really want another job, but I did want money to buy the things I needed and to support my social life. The problem was that most jobs asked for both a college degree and a lot of skills. Even though I had some skills, I didn't have a college education. It's too bad I couldn't get paid for watching talk shows every morning.

8. **Back on Track**

Even though TV talk shows can fill up your day, I was bored and sinking deeper into depression. After a month or two of unemployment, I told myself that there was no way for me to have the things I want in life without college.

I realize now that I am cut out for college—just not the college I ended up at. Right now, I'm trying to get into a public school upstate. That way I'll be able to live on campus the way I always imagined I would. Now that I've experienced first-hand what's it's like to live in one place, work in another place and go to school someplace else, I'm more convinced than ever that I need to eat, sleep, and breathe college in order to succeed.

Troy's experience at Baruch College is dramatized in the DVD Alternative High. *He later got into a college that was a better fit for him, and graduated.*

Heading for the Unknown

Behind the Scenes with Troy Shawn Welcome

1. **A**s you see in the film, I dropped out of my first college, but I got into a more supportive college and graduated. I thought things would just get better after that. But other than the discussion in family group back in high school, I had never really dealt with my feelings toward my father.

Then some personal things started to happen. I had a relationship that ended. The anger I felt as a teen started to come back. I was depressed, probably for about six months. At one point I remembered the words of my high school counselor. He

---

The DVD Alternative High *tells the story of Troy Shawn Welcome, a former teen writer at Youth Communication and the author of several of the stories in this book. The film shows part of Troy's journey from high school dropout to high school principal. Behind the scenes, he shared more about what happened next. This is some of what he had to say.*

always said that when things aren't going well, you need to find someone to talk to.

I found a therapist. I saw her for a couple years. I never really connected with her, but she still helped me. One day she said, "Why don't you look for your father?"

"Look for my father?! Why would I do that?"

"Because you seem to have a lot of anger that really belongs to him, but you're not directing it towards him. It's getting directed at yourself and everyone else in your life."

2. Understanding My Anger

That was true. I pretty much woke up angry. I was really displacing my anger in so many different ways, shooting it out at everyone except the person it really belonged with.

She said I needed to place my anger where it belongs. I started thinking back to every time I was just ready to pound someone or blow up. The intensity of my anger was always out of proportion to the situation. The underlying anger toward my father was coming out in other situations. It was hurting my relationships and could hurt my career.

I looked for my father. It had been years since we had any communication, but I found the number easily. In the end, we didn't reconnect. It just wasn't possible. But therapy helped me understand where my anger was coming from.

3. Talking It Out

Talking is one of the most important things—just being able to get it out. And you don't always want to have this kind of talk with your friends. I know a lot of people think, "Well, my friends are the only people I can talk to." But if your friends are stuck in the same place then they can't be that much help. They need help, too.

And sometimes it's important to be able to talk to someone who doesn't really know you, who is more objective, and who won't judge you the way your friends might, or feel threatened if you start to change. It can also be easier to hear something that you may not want to hear about yourself when it's from a stranger.

Most young men, and men in general, think that talking about your feelings is just not very manly. I mean, you don't get street cred for saying something like "Oh, I'm feeling kind of sad today," or "I want a hug." That just isn't the reality.

But I think it needs to become a reality. As men we tend to hold onto things and think that we are solving them by acting out, getting angry, and getting violent. We're acting out because

of emotions we're not aware of. I know I did. As men, we need to release our minds and our souls from this slave state where we're imprisoned by the emotions we can't express.

4. **Strength**

One of the things I try to get across to my young men is that facing emotions takes strength and courage. It takes courage to begin to see the behaviors that are keeping you in a negative cycle. It's very hard to see it. It's hard to recognize the patterns in your life and to acknowledge them.

If you keep running into the same kind of obstacles, it's because you're not facing your problems and you're not learning from them. You're just doing the same thing over and over, even though it's not working. You're walking into each situation without stopping to examine it, or asking yourself what would be the best way to react.

5. **Leaving Your Comfort Zone**

If you keep doing the same thing—if you keep choosing to turn right at every corner, and every time you get slapped in the face, then how about you turn left for once? Take the path that you haven't taken before and see what happens.

If you can, do something like go away to college. Leave everything behind. Leave behind your comfort zone, leave behind your friends. In the film, Jamie and the other guys were my comfort zone. It was hard, but I had to tell them, "I gotta go! I gotta go; I can't mess with you all, I can't do it. I'm tired."

It took me a long time to get that courage. At one point, probably just in time, I realized—by the grace of God or something—I realized I *have* to say no to my friends, I have to disconnect from them in some way. Not disrespect them, but I had to say, "I got some stuff to do so y'all do *you*, I gotta do *me*, and we're going to catch up in a little time. But I can't do *this* right now."

6. **The Risk to Change**

It was hard because running with them was fun and comfortable. Running with them made me feel safe, even though I wasn't. These are your boys, your peoples. You rock with them. It distracts you from all the things that really bother you, things that make you feel weak or scared or lonely. You know what I mean? You don't have to pay attention to any of that when you're with your boys, because you're doing exciting things that block out any bad or scary feelings.

But if you want to change, you have to be in a mental place where you start to feel a little weak (or scared or lonely). Because learning how to deal with your real feelings is the only thing that makes you a stronger man in the long run.

It's funny. How could being weak make you strong? It's  because when you're looking at those two doors, one that's familiar and one that's unknown...if you have the courage to head in the direction [of the] unknown...man, your life begins to open up in some amazing ways. Suddenly you realize—"Wait, my life can actually be *intentional*—what I want to make it."

7. **Don't Be Passive**

I'm sure you've heard people say, "When things are going good, you know something's going to go bad." My friend Eric in the film always used to say that. People who believe that are passive. They believe they are controlled by their environment. The reality is, you're not.

You don't need to wait for life to do something *to* you. You need to do something with life. That happens only when you begin to take the road that is difficult, the road that makes you fearful, that makes you vulnerable. The road you don't know how to control because it's not the streets.

It's new, and you have to begin to walk it slowly and pay attention to every step. And which direction you're going in. And what happens every time you run into a different wall. You begin to come out of autopilot; you begin to dictate what your life will be. You begin to create your own destiny.

8. **Getting from Here to There**

At first, you don't even have to have a goal. You just want to take a walk in the direction that is going to be good for you. That's all. That's the only goal you need—to do something that's going to be good for you, or to just avoid a bad place.

You have to believe that you can have a future, you have to want it. Too many of us, in the urban world, believe that the streets we walk every day and the set battles we have, one block against another—that that's all it's about. It can be all about that if the endpoint is only going to be you ending up in jail or dead or regretful. But then it's not good for you. So you have to begin to accept that there is something else that is good for you.

9. **It's Not Easy**

I say it like it's an easy thing but it's not an easy thing. Because if you live in a world like I did, it's governed by hate and anger and everything that's been done wrong to you and all the ways in which you weren't brought up that you really should have been.

You should have been brought up to understand that any-thing is possible. You should have been brought up to understand that you can create your own reality.

Eric used to believe he'd be dead by the time he was like 21. If you believe that, then you do everything that's wrong for you, that's negative. You create that reality. If you believe that all that exists for you is the street and the guns and the drugs and the battling and death—if that's what you believe, then you're creating that.

You can speak and think a different reality into existence, so start.

10. **The Hardest Part**

But the hardest thing with that is you don't know. You don't know and you're afraid that people are going to see parts of you that even you aren't comfortable seeing.

You're nervous, you're filled with anxiety, you keep wanting to just go back to the thing you know. The place that feels safe. And then you start to lie to yourself, telling yourself that it's the "wrong time" to do something unknown. You tell yourself you need to have a guarantee, a certain thing.

But you don't. And I think the way that you deal with it is by accepting how you feel. Accept that you feel nervous; it's OK. When you feel nervous and insecure and weak, don't jump into something that will make you feel stronger. Don't try to compensate for it. You feel nervous. Talk about it with someone you trust. Or, if you can't, say it to yourself, "All right, I'm nervous, I'm a little scared, all right." Acknowledge it, and it won't have so much power over you.

And once you accept it, don't punish yourself for feeling weak. Once you feel you don't have to justify these things about yourself, then you can begin to move forward, one step at a time. Take your time. Make each decision as you need to. Soon, that thing that's strange will start to feel somewhat familiar. You start to create the other side of you. The side that welcomes challenges and differences. The side that is excited by something new that you don't know. And then you start to realize how amazing a person you really are.

About Youth Communication

Youth Communication, founded in 1980, is nonprofit educational publishing company located in New York City. Our mission is to help marginalized youth develop their full potential through reading and writing, so that they can succeed in school and at work and contribute to their communities.

Youth Communication publishes true stories by teens that are developed in a rigorous writing program. We offer more than 50 books that adults can use to engage reluctant teen readers on an array of topics including peer pressure, school, sex, and relationships. Our stories also appear in our two award-winning magazines, **YC**_teen_ and _Represent_, and on our website (www.youthcomm.org), and are frequently reprinted in popular and professional magazines and textbooks. We offer hundreds of lessons, complete leader's guides (like this one) and professional development to help educators use the stories to help teens improve their academic, social, and emotional skills.

Our stories, written by a diverse group of writers, are uniquely compelling to peers who do not see their experiences reflected in mainstream reading materials. They motivate teens to read and write, encourage good values, and show teens how to make positive changes in their lives.

You can access many of our stories and sample lessons for free at www.youthcomm.org. For more information on our products and services, contact Loretta Chan at 212-279-0708 x115, or lchan@youthcomm.org.

Youth Communication ®
224 W. 29th St., 2nd fl.
New York, NY 10001

212-279-0708
www.youthcomm.org

The Real Stories Program

Real Stories is the umbrella name for a series of programs that promote reading, social and emotional development, and the knowledge and skills young people need to succeed. The program is aimed at middle and high school students—especially those who are resistant to reading. The entire series is built around true stories by teens in the Youth Communication writing program. The stories are paired with experiential activities that reinforce the themes of the stories.

The first program in the series, *Real Stories, Real Teens*, focuses on general themes of youth development and identity. It also promotes extended reading through the inclusion of novels from the Bluford High School series. *Real Stories, Real Teens* is designed to be used in out-of-school time settings like after school and summer programs. It is also suitable in advisories or in-school classes where teens are very resistant to reading.

It consists of an anthology with 26 true stories by teens and three fiction excerpts, a detailed Leader's Guide with 28 experiential workshops, and a dozen Bluford novels. *Real Stories, Real Teens* won the 2008 award for best curriculum in its class from the Association of Educational Publishers.

The second program in the series, *Real Jobs, Real Stories*, is focused on work readiness for teens. It is designed to help teens find and succeed in their first jobs. The *Real Jobs* program consists of an anthology of 33 true stories, an extensive Leader's Guide, and a 32-page workbook. The Leader's Guide includes 21 hours of experiential workshops with dozens of activities.

The third program in the series, *Real Men*, focuses on the experiences of young men of color and the struggle to figure out what it means to be a man. It includes an anthology (the book you're holding) of true stories, an extensive Leader's Guide, and a 15-minute DVD about one young man's journey from high school dropout to high school principal.

Reading the stories in the *Real Stories* program, talking about them with peers, and engaging in the activities from the Leader's Guides helps young people explore ideas and values, engage in healthy discussion, and reflect on their own lives and choices.

In many of the stories, the writers describe how they coped with significant challenges. The activities in the Leader's Guide help teens imagine how they would manage similar challenges (or avoid them in the first place). The activities also show teens how they can be helpful and supportive of their peers.

A key benefit of the *Real Stories* program is that it makes reading an enriching and rewarding experience. Unlike traditional reading programs, *Real Stories* engages hard-to-reach teens by providing them with peer-written stories that speak to their experience and model good choices and values. That helps build teens' motivation to read, while strengthening their skills.

To order more copies of **Real Men, Real Stories**,
The Leader's Guide to Real Men, Real Stories,
or the DVD **Alternative High**, go to
www.youthcomm.org or call
212-279-0708 x115.

For information about training and professional
development, contact Loretta Chan at 212-279-0708
x115 or lchan@youthcomm.org

Credits

The stories in this book originally appeared in the following Youth Communication publications:

"Deciding My Own Worth," by Juelz Long, *New Youth Connections*, May/June 2006; "Step-Family Ties," by Jordan Temple, *New Youth Connections*, November 2008; "My Father: I Want To Be Everything He's Not," by Troy Shawn Welcome, *New Youth Connections*, May/June 1994; "Back in Touch," by Eric Benson, *Risemagazine.org*, June 2009; "My Father, My Friend," by Macario DeLaCruz, *New Youth Connections*, September/October 2001; "My Street Brothers," by Derrick B., *Represent*, September/October 2007; "Hear No Evil, See No Evil...Do No Evil," by Curtis Holmes, *New Youth Connections*, September/October 1998; "Goodbye, Harlem," by Antwaun Garcia, *Represent*, March/April 2006; "Following the Leader," by Anonymous, *Represent*, March/April 2006; "Crewsin' for a Bruisin'," by Troy Shawn Welcome, *New Youth Connections*, April 1994; "Color Me Different," by Jamal Greene, *New Youth Connections*, September/October 1994; "Getting Ghetto," by Fred Wagenhauser, *Represent*, May/June 2007; "I'm Not What You Expect Me to Be," by Jordan Yue, *New Youth Connections*, January/February 2004; "The Soundtrack of My Life," by Otis Hampton, *Represent*, Fall 2010; "Gay in Da Hood," by Jeremiyah D. Spears, *Represent*, January/February 2000; "Clean and Kind of Sober," by Antwaun Garcia, *Represent*, May/June 2005; "Letting It Out," by Ashunte Hunt, *Represent*, September/October 2007; "Karate Killed the Monster Inside Me," by Robin Chan, *New Youth Connections*, November 1996;

Credits

"Don't Keep it Inside: Talk it Out," by Norman B., *New Youth Connections*, November 1997; "Will the Tortoise Win the Race?" by Eric Green, *Represent*, March/April 2005; "No More Hand-Holding," by Edgar Lopez, *New Youth Connections*, September/October 2008; "Community College: A Second Chance," by Jordan Temple, *New Youth Connections*, September/October 2008; "Freshman Year Is a Fresh Start," by Ferentz Lafargue, *New Youth Connections*, April 1995; "It Wasn't Easy, But I Did It: How I Found My Job," by Sharif Berkeley, *Represent*, July/August 1995; "Going Back to Preschool," by Gamal Jones, *New Youth Connections*, April 2007; "Young and Hungry," by Joseph Alvarez, *Represent*, March/April 2006; "Maxed Out," by Xavier Reyes, *Represent*, November/December 2005; "Building Trust, Brick by Brick," by Manny, *Represent*, March/April 2008; "Opening Up to My Shorty," by Antwaun Garcia, *Represent*, January/February 2003; "I Have Faith in My Church," by Stephen Simpson, *New Youth Connections*, December 1998; "Some POPS Are Hanging In," by Antwaun Garcia, *Represent*, March/April 2005; "Becoming a Father," by Michael Orr, *Represent*, May/June 2009; "My School Is Like a Family," by Troy Shawn Welcome, *New Youth Connections*, May/June 1994; "My First Semester: Overworked, Underpaid, and Unprepared," by Troy Shawn Welcome, *New Youth Connections*, April 1995.

Story Index by Theme

Story Index by Theme

About the Writers

The Teen Writers: The true stories in *Real Men, Real Stories* were written by teens in Youth Communication's intensive writing workshops. Teens participate in the workshops to improve their skills, learn about themselves, and write stories that will benefit their peers and the adults who work with them. Today, many of these young writers are continuing to make important contributions to their communities. Many have gone on to become teachers, principals, police officers, journalists, environmental activists, social workers, and college professors.

About the Editors

Laura Longhine is the editorial director at Youth Communication. She edits youthsuccessnyc.org, a website for youth aging out of foster care in New York, and has edited several other Youth Communication anthologies for teens. She previously edited *Represent*, Youth Communication's magazine by and for youth in foster care. She has a bachelor's degree in English from Tufts University and a master's in journalism from Columbia University.

Keith Hefner co-founded Youth Communication in 1980 and has directed it ever since. He is the recipient of the Luther P. Jackson Education Award from the New York Association of Black Journalists and a MacArthur Fellowship. He was also a Revson Fellow at Columbia University. He has written and tested curriculum that accompanies Youth Communication's teen-written books and magazines for more than 20 years.

Other Helpful Books
From Youth Communication

 *Finding My Way: Minority Teens Write About College.* These writers, all racial and ethnic minorities, show how to succeed on campus, and describe how the racial make-up of a college affects their experience.

Growing Up Black: Teens Write About African-American Identity. Your teens will want to share their own experiences when they read these true stories about family, friendship, sexuality, popular culture, city life, hair, and yes, racism.

 Boys to Men: Teens Write About Becoming a Man. The young men in this book write about confronting the challenges of growing up. Their honesty and courage make them role models for teens who are bombarded with contradictory messages about what it means to be a man. (Youth Communication)

The Fury Inside: Teens Write About Anger. Help teens manage their anger. These writers show how they got better control of their emotions and sought the support of others. (Youth Communication)

 Real Jobs, Real Stories. Help teens identify and strengthen the skills they need to succeed in the workplace, while building their literacy skills and motivation to read. (Youth Communication)

Real Stories, Real Teens. Inspire teens to read and recognize their strengths with this collection of 26 true stories by teens. The young writers describe how they overcame significant challenges and stayed true to themselves. Also includes the first chapters from three novels in the Bluford Series. (Youth Communication)

Growing Up Latino: Teens Write About Hispanic-American Identity. What does it mean to be a Latino teen? Spur a discussion with these stories about real experiences with family, ethnic pride, and cultural conflict. (Youth Communication)

Dealing With Dad: Teens Write About Their Fathers. This book will help teens better understand and appreciate their own experiences growing up with and without their fathers. Boys and girls write about all kinds of fathers: the loving father, the distant father, the absent father, and the father they've never met. (Youth Communication)

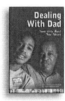

In Too Deep: Teens Write About Gangs. Teens write candidly about the impact of gang violence on their lives and community, including friends who were murdered. Some describe how they left gangs and turned their lives around. (Youth Communication)

Growing Up Girl: Young Women Write About Their Lives. The often troubling transition from girlhood to womanhood is examined as girls speak out about gender inequities, fashion, sex and relationships, family expectations, and more in 16 compelling stories. (Youth Communication)

Growing Up Muslim-American: Stories by Muslim Youth. Teens of all backgrounds will appreciate these true stories that tackle the issues of invisibility, discrimination, arranged marriage, and pride in the Muslim faith. (Youth Communication)

To order these and other books, go to:
www.youthcomm.org
or call 212-279-0708 x115

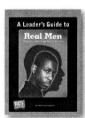

CPSIA information can be obtained at www.ICGtesting.com
Printed in the USA
267502BV00002B/4/P

9 781935 552437